THE MAN
WITHOUT
CONTENT

MERIDIAN

Crossing Aesthetics

Werner Hamacher

& David E. Wellbery

Editors

Translated by
Georgia Albert

Stanford
University
Press

———

Stanford
California

THE MAN WITHOUT CONTENT

Giorgio Agamben

The Man Without Content
was originally published in Italian in 1994
under the title *L'uomo senza contenuto*
© 1994 by Quodlibet for the Italian edition

Stanford University Press
Stanford, California

© 1999 by the Board of Trustees
of the Leland Stanford Junior University

Printed in the United States of America

CIP data appear at the end of the book

To Giovanni Urbani
as a token of friendship and gratitude

Contents

Translator's Note

The Man Without Content engages in a dialogue with a large number of literary and especially philosophical figures, from Plato to Walter Benjamin. With the exception of the Greek and French sources, Agamben quotes in Italian translation, frequently his own. In the instances in which I have located English translations for the passages quoted, I have routinely modified them to follow more closely the wording of Agamben's Italian translations. In cases where no published translation is cited, the translations are mine.

Thanks to Thomas Albrecht, David Arndt, Jennifer Bajorek, E. S. Burt, Erin Ferris, Kevin Newmark, Richard Regosin, and Elizabeth Rottenberg for help with sources, and to Nancy Young for her excellent editing.

THE MAN
WITHOUT
CONTENT

§ 1 The Most Uncanny Thing

In the third essay of the *Genealogy of Morals,* Nietzsche subjects the Kantian definition of the beautiful as disinterested pleasure to a radical critique:

> Kant thought he was honoring art when among the predicates of beauty he emphasized and gave prominence to those which established the honor of knowledge: impersonality and universality. This is not the place to inquire whether this was essentially a mistake; all I wish to underline is that Kant, like all philosophers, instead of envisaging the aesthetic problem from the point of view of the artist (the creator), considered art and the beautiful purely from that of the "spectator," and unconsciously introduced the "spectator" into the concept "beautiful." It would not have been so bad if this "spectator" had at least been sufficiently familiar to the philosophers of beauty—namely, as a great *personal* fact and experience, as an abundance of vivid authentic experiences, desires, surprises, and delights in the realm of the beautiful! But I fear that the reverse has always been the case; and so they have offered us, from the beginning, definitions in which, as in Kant's famous definition of the beautiful, a lack of any refined first-hand experience reposes in the shape of a fat worm of error. "That is beautiful," said Kant, "which gives us pleasure *without interest.*" Without interest! Compare with this definition one framed by a genuine "spectator" and artist—Stendhal, who once called the beautiful *une promesse de bonheur.* At any rate he *rejected* and repudiated the one point about

the aesthetic condition which Kant had stressed: *le désinteressement.*
Who is right, Kant or Stendhal?

If our aestheticians never weary of asserting in Kant's favor that, under the spell of beauty, one can *even* view undraped female statues
"without interest," one may laugh a little at their expense: the experiences of *artists* on this ticklish point are more "interesting," and Pygmalion was in any event *not* necessarily an "unaesthetic man."[1]

The experience of art that is described in these words is in no way
an *aesthetics* for Nietzsche. On the contrary: the point is precisely
to purify the concept of "beauty" by filtering out the αἴσθησις, the
sensory involvement of the spectator, and thus to consider art from
the point of view of its creator. This purification takes place as a reversal of the traditional perspective on the work of art: the aesthetic
dimension—the sensible apprehension of the beautiful object on
the part of the spectator—is replaced by the creative experience of
the artist who sees in his work only *une promesse de bonheur,* a
promise of happiness. Having reached the furthest limit of its destiny in the "hour of the shortest shadow," art leaves behind the
neutral horizon of the aesthetic and recognizes itself in the "golden
ball" of the will to power. Pygmalion, the sculptor who becomes
so enamored of his creation as to wish that it belonged no longer to
art but to life, is the symbol of this turn from the idea of disinterested beauty as a denominator of art to the idea of happiness, that
is, of an unlimited growth and strengthening of the vital values,
while the focal point of the reflection on art moves from the disinterested spectator to the interested artist.

In foreseeing this change, Nietzsche was a good prophet as usual.
If one compares what he writes in the third essay of the *Genealogy
of Morals* with the terms Antonin Artaud uses in the preface to
Theater and Its Double to describe the agony of Western culture,
one notices, precisely on this point, a surprising agreement in their
views. "It is our occidental idea of art that has caused us to lose culture. . . . To our inert and disinterested idea of art an authentic culture opposes a violently egoistic and magical, i.e., *interested* idea."[2]
In a sense, the idea that art is not a disinterested experience was
perfectly familiar in other eras. When Artaud, in "Theater and

Plague," remembers the decree issued by Scipio Nasica, the grand pontiff who had the Roman theaters razed, and the fury with which Saint Augustine attacks the "scenic games," responsible for the death of the soul, one can hear in his words the nostalgia that a soul such as his, who thought that theater drew its only worth "from an excruciating magical relation to reality and danger," must have felt for a time that had such a concrete and interested notion of the theater as to deem it necessary to destroy it for the health of soul and city. It is no doubt superfluous to note that today it would be impossible to find such ideas even among censors. However, it may be useful to point out that the first time that something similar to an autonomous examination of the aesthetic phenomenon appears in European medieval society, it takes the form of aversion and repugnance toward art, in the instructions given by those bishops who, faced with the musical innovations of the *ars nova*, prohibited the modulation of the song and the *fractio vocis* during the religious services because they distracted the faithful with their charm. Thus, among the statements in favor of interested art, Nietzsche might have cited a passage in Plato's *Republic* that is often invoked when speaking about art, even though this has not made the paradoxical attitude that is expressed there any less scandalous to the modern ear. Plato, as is well known, sees the poet as a danger and a cause of ruin for the city:

> If a man who was capable by his cunning of assuming every kind of shape and imitating all things should arrive in our city, bringing with himself the poems which he wished to exhibit, we should fall down and worship him as a holy and wondrous and delightful creature, but should say to him that there is no man of that kind among us in our city, nor is it lawful for such a man to arise among us, and we should send him away to another city, after pouring myrrh down over his head and crowning him with fillets of wood.

"We can admit no poetry into our city," adds Plato with an expression that shocks our aesthetic sensibility, "save only hymns to the gods and the praises of good men."[3]

Even before Plato, however, a condemnation of art, or at least a suspicious stance toward it, had already been expressed in the words of a poet, namely Sophocles, at the end of the first stasimon of his *Antigone*. After characterizing man, insofar as he is the one who has τέχνη (that is, in the broad meaning the Greeks gave this term, the ability to pro-duce, to bring a thing from nonbeing into being), as the most uncanny thing there is, the chorus continues by saying that this power can lead to happiness as easily as to ruin, and concludes with a wish that recalls the Platonic ban on poets: "Not by my fire, / never to share my thoughts, who does these things."[4]

Edgar Wind has observed that the reason why Plato's statement is so surprising to us is that art does not exert the same influence on us as it did on him.[5] Only because art has left the sphere of *interest* to become merely *interesting* do we welcome it so warmly. In a draft of *The Man Without Qualities* that Robert Musil wrote at a time when the definitive design of his novel was not yet clear in his mind, Ulrich (who still appears with his earlier name, Anders) enters the room where Agathe is playing the piano and feels an obscure and irresistible impulse that drives him to fire some gun shots at the instrument that is diffusing through the house such a "desolatingly" beautiful harmony. As for us, however, it is likely that if we attempted to go to the bottom of the peaceful contemplation that we, unlike Ulrich, usually reserve for works of art, we would eventually find ourselves in agreement with Nietzsche, who thought that his time had no right to answer Plato's question about art's moral influence, since "even if we had the art—where do we see the influence, *any* influence from art?"[6] Plato, and Greek classical antiquity in general, had a very different experience of art, an experience having little to do with disinterest and aesthetic enjoyment. The power of art over the soul seemed to him so great that he thought it could by itself destroy the very foundations of his city; but nonetheless, while he was forced to banish it, he did so reluctantly, "since we ourselves are very conscious of her spell."[7] The term he uses when he wants to define the effects of inspired imagination is θεῖος φοβός, "divine terror," a term that we, benevolent spectators, no doubt find inappropriate to define our reactions, but that nevertheless is found with increasing frequency, after a certain time, in the notes in which modern artists attempt to capture their experience of art.

It appears, in fact, that simultaneously with the process through which the spectator insinuates himself into the concept of "art," confining it to the τόπος οὐράνιος, the heavenly place, of aesthetics, we see the opposite process taking place from the point of view of the artist. For the one who creates it, art becomes an increasingly uncanny experience, with respect to which speaking of interest is at the very least a euphemism, because what is at stake seems to be not in any way the production of a beautiful work but instead the life and death of the author, or at least his or her spiritual health. To the increasing innocence of the spectator's experience in front of the beautiful object corresponds the increasing danger inherent in the artist's experience, for whom art's *promesse de bonheur* becomes the poison that contaminates and destroys his existence. The idea that extreme risk is implicit in the artist's activity begins to gain currency, almost as though—so thought Baudelaire—it were a sort of duel to the death "où l'artiste crie de frayeur avant d'être vaincu" ("where the artist cries out in fright before being defeated"); and to prove how little this idea is merely one metaphor among those forming the "properties" of the "literary histrio," it suffices to quote what Hölderlin wrote on the brink of madness: "I fear that I might end like the old Tantalus who received more from the Gods than he could take," and "I may say that Apollo struck me."[8] Or the note found in Van Gogh's pocket on the day of his death: "Well, as for my own work, I risk my life in it and my sanity has already half melted away in it." Or Rilke, in a letter to Clara Rilke: "Works of art are always the product of a risk one has run, of an experience taken to its extreme limit, to the point where man can no longer go on."

Another notion that we encounter more and more frequently in artists' opinions is that art is something fundamentally dangerous not only for the one who produces it but for society as well. Hölderlin, in the notes in which he attempts to condense the meaning of his unfinished tragedy, finds a close connection, almost a unity, between the principle of the Agrigentans' anarchic unbridledness and Empedocles' titanic poetry; and he appears, in a projected hymn, to consider art the essential cause that led to the ruin of Greece:

> for they wanted to found
> a kingdom of art. But they missed
> the national [*das Vaterländische*] in the attempt
> and wretchedly
> Greece, the highest beauty, was ruined.[9]

And it is likely that in all of modern literature neither Monsieur Teste, nor Werf Rönne, nor Adrian Leverkühn would disagree with him, but only a character with such seemingly hopeless bad taste as Romain Rolland's Jean Christophe.

Everything, then, leads one to think that if today we gave the artists themselves the task of judging whether art should be allowed in the city, they would judge from their own experience and agree with Plato on the necessity of banishing it. If this is true, then the entrance of art into the aesthetic dimension—and the understanding of it starting from the αἴσθησις of the spectator—is not as innocent and natural a phenomenon as we commonly think. Perhaps nothing is more urgent—if we really want to engage the problem of art in our time—than a *destruction* of aesthetics that would, by clearing away what is usually taken for granted, allow us to bring into question the very meaning of aesthetics as the science of the work of art. The question, however, is whether the time is ripe for such a *destruction*, or whether instead the consequence of such an act would not be the loss of any possible horizon for the understanding of the work of art and the creation of an abyss in front of it that could only be crossed with a radical leap. But perhaps just such a loss and such an abyss are what we most need if we want the work of art to reacquire its original stature. And if it is true that the fundamental architectural problem becomes visible only in the house ravaged by fire, then perhaps we are today in a privileged position to understand the authentic significance of the Western aesthetic project.

Fourteen years before Nietzsche published the third essay of the *Genealogy of Morals*, a poet, whose word remains inscribed like a Medusa's head in the destiny of Western art, had asked poetry neither to produce beautiful works nor to respond to a disinterested aesthetic ideal, but to change man's life and reopen the gates of Eden for him. In this experience, in which *la magique étude du bonheur* (the magical study of happiness) obscures all other design to the point of becoming the sole fatality of poetry and life, Rimbaud had encountered Terror. Thus the "embarkation for the island of Cythera" of modern art was to lead the artist not to the promised happiness but to a competition with the Most Uncanny, with the divine terror that had driven Plato to banish the poets from his city. Only if understood as the final moment of this ongoing process, through which art purifies itself of the spectator to find itself faced by an absolute threat, does Nietzsche's invocation in the preface to the *Gay Science* acquire all its enigmatic meaning: "Ah, if you could really understand why we of all people need art . . . ," but "another kind of art . . . an art for artists, for artists only!"[10]

§ 2 Frenhofer and His Double

How can art, this most innocent of occupations, pit man against Terror? In *Les fleurs de Tarbes*, Jean Paulhan takes as his premise a fundamental ambiguity in language—namely, the fact that it is constituted on the one hand by signs that are perceived by the senses, and on the other by ideas associated with these signs in such a way as to be immediately evoked by them—and makes a distinction between two kinds of writers. There are the Rhetoricians, who dissolve all meaning into form and make form into the sole law of literature, and the Terrorists, who refuse to bend to this law and instead pursue the opposite dream of a language that would be nothing but meaning, of a thought in whose flame the sign would be fully consumed, putting the writer face to face with the Absolute. The Terrorist is a misologist, and does not recognize in the drop of water that remains on his fingertips the sea in which he thought he had immersed himself; the Rhetorician looks to the words and appears to distrust thought.

That the work of art is something other than what is simple in it is almost too obvious. This is what the Greeks expressed with the concept of allegory: the work of art ἄλλο ἀγορεύει, communicates something else, is something other than the material that contains it.[1] But there are objects—for example, a block of stone, a drop of water, and generally all natural objects—in which form seems to be determined and almost canceled out by matter, and other objects—a vase, a spade, or any other man-made object—in which form seems to be what determines matter. The dream of the Terror is to create works that are in the world in the same way as the block of stone or the drop of water; it is the dream of a *product* that exists according to the statute of the *thing*. "Les chefs-d'oeuvres sont bêtes," wrote Flaubert; "ils ont la mine tranquille comme les productions mêmes de la nature, comme les grands animaux et les montagnes" ("Masterpieces are stupid: they have placid faces like the very products of nature, like big animals and mountains"); and Degas, Valéry writes, used to say "C'est plat comme la belle peinture!" ("It's just as dull as beautiful painting!").[2]

The painter Frenhofer, in Balzac's *The Unknown Masterpiece*, is the perfect type of the Terrorist. Frenhofer has attempted for ten years to create on his canvas something that would not be just a work of art, albeit that of a genius; like Pygmalion, he has erased art with art to make out of his *Swimmer* not an assemblage of signs and colors but the living reality of his thought and his imagination. He tells his two visitors, "My painting [*ma peinture*] is not a painting, but a feeling, a passion! Born in my studio, it [*elle*] must remain here as a virgin and not leave if not covered." And later: "You are in front of a woman, and you are looking for a picture. There is such depth on this canvas, its air is so true, that you can't distinguish it from the air that surrounds us. Where is art? Lost, vanished!" But in this quest for absolute meaning, Frenhofer has succeeded only in obscuring his idea and erasing from the canvas any human form, disfiguring it into "a chaos of colors, tones, hesitating nuances, a kind of shapeless fog." In front of this absurd wall of paint, the young Poussin's cry—"but sooner or later he will have to realize that there is nothing on his canvas!"—sounds like an alarm responding to the threat that the Terror starts posing for Western art.[3]

But let us take a second look at Frenhofer's painting. On the canvas there is only a confused mass of colors contained inside a jumble of indecipherable lines. All meaning has been dissolved, all content has vanished, except the tip of a foot that stands out from the rest of the canvas "like the torso of a Venus sculpted in Paros marble standing among the ruins of a city destroyed by fire" (*Chef d'oeuvre*, p. 305). The quest for absolute meaning has devoured all meaning, allowing only signs, meaningless forms, to survive. But, then, isn't the unknown masterpiece instead the masterpiece of Rhetoric? Has the meaning erased the sign, or has the sign abolished the meaning? And here the Terrorist comes face to face with the paradox of the Terror. In order to leave the evanescent world of forms, he has no other means than form itself, and the more he wants to erase it, the more he has to concentrate on it to render it permeable to the inexpressible content he wants to express. But in the attempt, he ends up with nothing in his hands but signs— signs that, although they have traversed the limbo of non-meaning, are no less extraneous to the meaning he was pursuing. Fleeing from Rhetoric has led him to the Terror, but the Terror brings him back to its opposite, Rhetoric. Thus misology has to turn itself over into philology, and sign and meaning chase each other in a perpetual vicious circle.

The couple signifier-signified is, in fact, so indissolubly part of our linguistic heritage—of our language conceived metaphysically as φωνή σημαντική, as signifying sound—that any attempt to get over it without moving at the same time beyond the limits of metaphysics is destined to fall short of its aim. Modern literature offers all too many examples of this paradoxical destiny awaiting the Terror. The whole man of the Terror is also an *homme-plume*, and it is not useless to recall that one of the purest interpreters of the Terror in literature, Mallarmé, is also the one who made the book into the most perfect universe. Artaud, in the last years of his life, wrote some texts, called *Suppôts et fragmentations* (Henchmen and fragmentations), in which he intended to dissolve literature entirely into something he had at other times called the theater in the sense in which the alchemists called *Theatrum Chemicum* the description of their spiritual itinerary, a sense to which we do not come an inch closer when we think of the current meaning of the word "theater" in Western culture. But what has produced this voyage beyond literature, if not signs whose meaninglessness makes us ask questions precisely because we feel that in these signs someone sought, to the last, the destiny of literature? The only gesture available to the Terror that really wants to reduce itself to its ultimate coherence is that of Rimbaud, the gesture with which, as Mallarmé put it, he surgically removed poetry from himself while alive. But the paradox of the Terror is still present even in this extreme move. For what is the mystery we call Rimbaud if not the point where literature annexes its opposite, namely, silence? Isn't Rimbaud's fame divided, as Blanchot rightly observed, between "the poems that he wrote and those that he did not deign to write?"[4] And isn't this the masterpiece of Rhetoric? One must ask at this point whether the opposition of Terror and Rhetoric may not conceal something more than an empty reflection on a perennial riddle, and whether the insistence with which modern art has remained entangled in it may reveal a phenomenon of a different kind.

What happens to Frenhofer? So long as no other eye contemplated his masterpiece, he did not doubt his success for one moment; but one look at the canvas through the eyes of his two spectators is enough for him to appropriate Porbus's and Poussin's opinion: "Nothing! Nothing! And I worked on this for ten years" (*Chef d'oeuvre*, p. 306). Frenhofer becomes double. He moves from the point of view of the artist to that of the spectator, from the interested *promesse de bonheur* to disinterested aesthetics. In this transition, the integrity of his work dissolves. For it is not only Frenhofer that becomes double, but his work as well; just as in some combinations of geometric figures, which, if observed for a long time, acquire a different arrangement, from which one cannot return to the previous one except by closing one's eyes, so his work alternately presents two sides that cannot be put back together into a unity. The side that faces the artist is the living reality in which he reads his promise of happiness; but the other side, which faces the spectator, is an assemblage of lifeless elements that can only mirror itself in the aesthetic judgment's reflection of it.

This doubling between art as it is lived by the spectator, on the one hand, and art as it is lived by the artist on the other is indeed Terror, and thus the opposition between Terror and Rhetoric brings us back to the opposition between artists and spectators from which we started. Aesthetics then not only would be the determination of the work of art starting from the αἴσθησις, from the sensible apprehension of the spectator, but also would include from the beginning an examination of the work of art as the *opus* of a particular and irreducible *operari* (working), the artistic *operari*. This duality of principles, according to which the work is determined starting both from the creative activity of the artist and from the sensible apprehension of the spectator, traverses the entire history of aesthetics, and it is probably in this duality that one must seek its speculative center and its vital contradiction. We are now perhaps ready to ask what Nietzsche meant to say when he spoke of an art for artists only. Is it, namely, simply a shift in the traditional point of view on art, or are we not rather in the presence of a transformation in the essential status of the work of art which could explain its present destiny?

§ 3 The Man of Taste and the Dialectic of the Split

Around the middle of the seventeenth century the figure of the *man of taste* makes its appearance in European society: the figure, that is, of the man who is endowed with a particular faculty, almost with a *sixth sense*—as they started to say then—which allows him to grasp the *point de perfection* that is characteristic of every work of art.[1]

La Bruyère's *Characters* registers the appearance of this figure as a by-now-familiar fact. This makes it all the more difficult, for the modern ear, to perceive what is unusual in the terms in which this disconcerting prototype of Western aesthetic man is presented. Writes La Bruyère:

> There is in art a point of perfection, as there is in Nature one of goodness and completeness. Anyone who feels this and loves it possesses a perfect taste; but he who is not sensible of it, and loves what is short of that point or beyond it, is wanting in taste. Thus there exists a good and a bad taste, and we are right in discussing the difference between them.[2]

To measure the extreme novelty of this figure, one has to recognize that even in the sixteenth century there was no clear boundary between good and bad taste, and that the experience of standing before a work of art and wondering about the correct way to understand it was not familiar even to the refined art lovers who commissioned work from Raphael or Michelangelo. The sensibility of the time did not see a great difference between works of sacred art and mechanical dolls, the *engins d'esbatement* and the colossal ornamental stands, full of automatons and live people, that served to animate the banquets of princes and popes. The very same artists whom we admire for their frescoes and their architectural masterpieces also took part in producing decorations of all kinds and projected machines such as the one invented by Brunelleschi—which represented the celestial sphere, surrounded by two rows of angels, from which an automaton (the Archangel Gabriel) took flight with the support of an almond-shaped mechanism—or such as the mechanical apparatuses, restored and painted by Melchior Broederlam, that sprayed the guests of Philip the Good with water and dust. Our aesthetic sensibility learns with horror that in the castle of Hesdin, in a hall decorated with a series of paintings representing the story of Jason, a series of machines was installed which, in addition to imitating Medea's spells, produced lightning, thunder, snow, and rain, to obtain a more realistic effect.

But when we move away from this masterpiece of confusion and bad taste and start examining more closely the figure of the man of taste, we are surprised to notice that his appearance does not correspond, as we might have expected, to the spirit's more receptive attitude toward art or even to an increased interest in art. The transformation that is taking place cannot be identified simply with a purification of the spectator's sensibility; rather, it involves and calls into question the very status of the work of art. Some Renaissance popes and nobles had made so much room for art in their lives that they neglected their responsibilities as statesmen in order to discuss with artists the planning and execution of their works. But if someone had said that their souls were endowed with a special organ to which was entrusted—to the exclusion of all other mental faculties and of any purely sensual interest—the identification and comprehension of the work of art, they would probably have judged this idea to be just as grotesque as if someone had claimed that man breathes not because his entire body needs it but only to satisfy his lungs.

And yet it is precisely such an idea that begins to spread with increasing authority in the cultivated society of seventeenth-century Europe. The very origin of the word "taste" seemed to suggest that, just as there was a healthy and a less healthy taste, there could also be good and not so good art. And the casualness with which the Italian author of one of the numerous treatises on the topic could affirm that "the term 'good taste,' which means to discern in a healthy fashion the good taste from the flawed in food, is found these days in the mouths of some people who attribute it to themselves in matters of human letters" already contains, in embryo, the idea that Valéry would wittily express almost three centuries later when he wrote, "le goût est fait de mille dégoûts" ("taste is made of a thousand distastes").[3]

The process leading to the identification of this mysterious organ devoted to the reception of the work of art could be compared to the three-quarter closing of a photo lens before a very bright object; and if one thinks of the blinding artistic blooming of the two previous centuries, this partial closing might even seem a necessary precaution. As the idea of taste increases in precision, and with it that particular kind of psychic reaction that will lead to the birth of that mystery of modern sensibility, the aesthetic judgment, the work of art (at least so long as it is not finished) starts to be regarded as the exclusive competence of the artist, whose creative imagination tolerates neither limits nor impositions. The non-artist, however, can only *spectare*, that is, transform himself into a less and less necessary and more and more passive partner, for whom the work of art is merely an occasion to practice his good taste. Our modern aesthetic education has accustomed us to finding this attitude normal and to resenting any intrusion into the artist's work as an unwarranted violation of his freedom. Certainly no modern Maecenas would dare meddle with the planning and execution of a commissioned work of art as much as the Cardinal Giulio de' Medici (later to become Pope Clement VII) meddled with those of the Sacrestia Nova in San Lorenzo; yet we know that Michelangelo not only did not show any irritation with it but in fact told one of his pupils that Clement VII had an exceptional understanding of the artistic process. On this topic, Edgar Wind recalls that the great patrons of the Renaissance were precisely what we believe patrons should never be, namely, "awkward and uncomfortable partners";[4] yet as late as 1855, Burkhardt could present the frescoes on the vault of the Sistine Chapel not only as the work of Michelangelo's genius but also as Pope Julius II's gift to humanity. "This work," he wrote in his *Cicerone*, "was due to Pope Julius II. By alternate pressure and concession, by contest and by kindness, he obtained what perhaps no one else could have done from Michelangelo. His memory deserves to be blessed by art."[5]

If, on the contrary, the man of taste of the seventeenth century, like the modern spectator, considers it to be evidence of bad taste to meddle in what the artist creates "out of whim or genius," this means, probably, that art does not occupy in his spiritual life the same place that it did in the life of Clement VII or Julius II.

The artist, faced with a spectator who becomes more similar to an evanescent ghost the more refined his taste becomes, moves in an increasingly free and rarefied atmosphere and begins the voyage that will take him from the live tissue of society to the hyperborean no-man's-land of aesthetics, in whose desert he will vainly seek nourishment and where he will eventually look like the Catoblepas in Flaubert's *Temptation of St. Anthony*, who devours his own extremities without realizing it.

For, while the balanced figure of the man of taste becomes widespread in European society, the artist enters a dimension of imbalance and eccentricity, thanks to which, after a rapid evolution, he will justify the *idée reçue* that Flaubert recorded in his *Dictionary of Received Ideas* at the entry "Artists": "Express surprise that they dress like everyone else."[6] The more that taste attempts to free art from all contamination and interference, the more impure and nocturnal becomes the face that it shows those who have to produce it; and it is certainly no accident that with the appearance of the type of the false genius in the course of the seventeenth century the figure of the artist starts to cast a shadow from which it will be impossible to separate in the following centuries.[7]

∽

Just like the artist, the man of taste has his shadow, and it is perhaps this shadow that we will have to interrogate now if we want to come closer to his mystery. The type of the man of bad taste (*mauvais goût*) is not a totally new figure in European society; however, during the course of the seventeenth century, just as the concept of good taste is forming, it acquires such weight and relief that we should not be surprised if it turned out that Valéry's judgment quoted above, that "taste is made of a thousand distastes," has to be understood in a completely unexpected way, namely, in the sense that *good taste is essentially made of bad taste*.

The man of bad taste, as is implicit in La Bruyère's definition, is not simply the one who, totally lacking the organ needed to be receptive to art, is blind to it or contemptuous of it: rather, the person of bad taste is the person who loves what is "short of the right point or beyond it," who does not know how to identify the *point de perfection* of the work of art by distinguishing truth from falsehood. Molière left a famous portrait of the man of bad taste in *Le bourgeois gentilhomme* (The would-be gentleman): Monsieur Jourdain is not contemptuous of art, nor can it be said that he is indifferent to its charm; on the contrary, his greatest wish is to be a man of good taste and to be able to distinguish the beautiful from the ugly, art from not-art. He is not only, as Voltaire said, "a bourgeois who wants to be a distinguished man [*homme de qualité*]"[8] but also a man of bad taste who wants to become a man of taste. This wish is already in itself a rather mysterious fact, because it is not clear how someone who has no taste might consider good taste to be something of value. But what is even more surprising is that in his comedy Molière seems to treat Monsieur Jourdain with a certain indulgence, as though his ingenuous bad taste seemed to him less extraneous to art than the refined but cynical and corrupt sensibility of the masters who are supposed to educate him and of the *hommes de qualité* who try to trick him. Rousseau, in spite of his belief that in his comedy Molière had taken sides for the *hommes de qualité*, noticed that in the playwright's eyes only Jourdain could be a positive character. He wrote in the *Letter to D'Alembert*: "I hear it said that [Molière] attacks the vices; but I should like those that he attacks to be compared with those he encourages. Who is more blameworthy, an unintelligent and vain bourgeois who foolishly plays the gentleman, or the rascally gentleman who fools him?"[9] But the paradox of Monsieur Jourdain is that he is not only more honest than his teachers but also, in some way, more sensitive and open toward the work of art than those who are supposed to teach him how to judge it. This boorish man is tormented by beauty; this illiterate man who does not know what prose is has such love for letters that the mere idea that what he says is in any case *prose* is capable of transfiguring him. His interest, which is unable to judge its object, is closer to art than that of men of taste, who, faced with his scarce intellectual capacities, think that his money can right his brain's judgment and that his purse has discernment. We are here in the presence of a very curious phenomenon, which precisely at this moment starts assuming macroscopic dimensions: it seems, that is, that art prefers to compose itself in the shapeless and undifferentiated mold of bad taste than to reflect itself in the precious crystal of good taste. Everything happens, that is, as though good taste, by enabling those who have it to perceive the *point de perfection* of the artwork, ended up by making them indifferent to it, or as if art, entering the perfect receptive mechanism of good taste, lost that vitality that a less perfect but more interested mechanism is on the contrary able to preserve.

But there is more. If the man of taste thinks about himself for a moment, he must notice not only that he has become indifferent to the work of art, but that the more his taste is purified, the more his soul is spontaneously attracted by everything that good taste cannot but condemn, as though good taste carried within itself a tendency to pervert itself into its opposite. The first recognition of this feature, which would later become one of the most obviously contradictory (but not on this account less unobserved) ones in our culture, is found in two surprising letters of Madame de Sevigné's, dated July 5 and 12, 1671. Speaking of the novels of intrigue, which were just starting to become popular with a restricted audience, this perfect woman of taste wonders how to explain the attraction she feels for such second-rate works:

I often wonder where the fancy I have for such ridiculous stuff could come from; I can hardly comprehend it. Perhaps you remember me enough to know how much bad style in writing displeases me; that I have some discernment for a good one; and that no person is more sensible to the charms of eloquence. La Calprenède's style is wretched in a thousand places; long-winded periods, ugly words; I feel all this. . . . I know, then, how detestable [La Calprenède's] style of writing is, yet I continue to get caught in it like a limed bird: the beauty of the sentiments, the violence of the passions, the greatness of the events, and the miraculous success of their redoubtable swords, I get carried away by all this like a little girl; I become a party in all their designs, and if I did not have M. de La Rochefoucauld and M. d'Hacqueville to comfort me, I would hang myself for being guilty of such a weakness.[10]

This inexplicable inclination of good taste toward its opposite has become so familiar to us moderns that we are not even surprised by it anymore, and we no longer even wonder (although it would be natural to do so) how it is possible that our taste is divided between objects as incompatible as the *Duino Elegies* and Ian Fleming's novels, Cézanne's canvases and knickknacks with floral patterns. When Brunetière, two centuries after Madame de Sevigné, again observes this reprehensible impulse of good taste, it has become so strong in the meantime that the critic, while maintaining the distinction between good and bad literature, almost has to force himself to avoid devoting himself exclusively to the latter:

What cruel destiny is the critic's! All other men follow the impulses of their tastes. He alone spends his time fighting his! If he gives way to his pleasure, a voice calls out to him: wretched man, what are you doing? What! *Le deux gosses* makes you cry and *Le plus heureux des trois* makes you laugh! Labiche amuses you and Dennery moves you! You hum Béranger's music! You secretly read Alexandre Dumas, perhaps, or Soulié! Where are your principles, your mission, your priesthood?[11]

In other words, a phenomenon takes place for the man of taste that is similar to the one Proust describes for the intelligent man, to whom "having become more intelligent gives the right to be less so." And just as it seems that intelligence, past a certain limit, needs stupidity, so one is tempted to say that, starting from a certain degree of refinement, good taste can no longer do without bad taste. Today the existence of an art and literature whose sole purpose is entertainment is so exclusively attributed to a mass society, and we are so accustomed to seeing it through the psychological condition of the intellectuals who witnessed its first explosion in the second half of the nineteenth century, that we forget that when it first arose, when Madame de Sevigné described its paradoxical fascination in La Calprenède's novels, it was an aristocratic, not a popular, phenomenon. And the critics of mass culture would certainly be setting themselves a more useful task if they started asking, first of all, how it could have happened that precisely a refined elite should have felt the need to create vulgar objects for its sensibility. After all, if we just look around, we notice that entertainment literature is again becoming today what it was at the origin, that is, a phenomenon that touches the higher layers of culture before the middle and lower ones; and it is certainly not to our honor that among the many intellectuals who devote themselves exclusively to kitsch and the feuilleton there is not a Madame de Sevigné willing to hang herself for her weakness.

As for the artists, it did not take them long to learn the lesson of La Calprenède's novels, and they started to introduce bad taste into the work of art, imperceptibly at first, then in a much more overt manner; they made the "beauty of the sentiments," the "violence of the passions" and the "miraculous success of . . . fearsome swords," and moreover all that could awaken and maintain the reader's interest, into one of the essential resources of literary fiction. The century that saw Frances Hutcheson and the other theoreticians of taste elaborate the ideal of uniformity and harmony as the essence of beauty also saw Giambattista Marino theorize his poetics of wonder and witnessed the excesses and extravagance of the Baroque as well. In the theater, the supporters of bourgeois tragedy and sentimental drama finally triumphed over their classicist opponents, and when Molière, in his *Monsieur de Pourceaugnac*, sought to represent two physicians attempting to give the protagonist an enema, he did not limit himself to bringing one cannula on the scene, but invaded the theater with them. The *genres tranchés* (distinct genres), the only ones admitted by the purists of taste, were gradually replaced by the less noble mixed genres. Their prototype was precisely the novel, which, born to satisfy the exigencies of bad taste, ended up occupying center stage in literary production. At the end of the eighteenth century there even appeared a new genre, the gothic romance, which was based on the simple reversal of the criteria of good taste, and the romantics, in their battle for an interested art, made use of this procedure without a second thought to regain for art, through disgust and terror, that area of the soul that good taste had deemed it necessary to exclude forever from aesthetic participation. This rebellion on the part of bad taste led to a real opposition between *poésie* on the one hand and *goût* (taste) or *esprit* (intelligence) on the other, so much so that a writer like Flaubert, who for his part never stopped being obsessed with emphasis and pompousness, was able to write in a letter to Louise Colet: "In order to have what one calls bad taste, one must have poetry in one's brain; the *esprit*, on the other hand, is incompatible with true poetry." It seems, that is, that genius and good taste cannot cohabit in the same brain, and that the artist, in order to be one, must first of all distinguish himself from the man of taste. In the meantime, Rimbaud's programmatic statement of bad taste in *Une saison en enfer* (A season in hell) has become so famous that we have difficulty noticing that it is possible to find in this list all the familiar equipment of the contemporary aesthetic consciousness:

> J'aimais les peintures idiotes, dessus de porte, décors, toiles de saltimbanques, enseignes, enluminures populaires; la littérature démodée, latin d'église, livres érotiques sans orthographe, romans de nos aïeules, contes de fées, petits livres de l'enfance, opéras vieux, refrains niais, rhythmes naïfs.[12]

> (I loved stupid pictures, the panels over doors, stage sets, the backdrops of mountebanks, inn signs, popular prints; antiquated literature, church Latin, badly spelled erotic books, the novels of our grandmothers, fairy tales, children's books, old operas, inane refrains and artless rhythms.)

From the point of view of taste, what was eccentric in Rimbaud's time has become something like the *average taste* of the intellectual, and has penetrated so deeply into the heritage of *bon ton* that it now constitutes a real mark of that heritage. Contemporary taste has rebuilt the castle of Hesdin; yet history does not offer return tickets, and before we enter the halls to admire what we are offered, we should perhaps reflect on this extraordinary practical joke played on us by our good taste.

~

Good taste does not simply have a tendency to pervert itself into its opposite; it is, in some way, the very principle of any perversion, and its appearance in consciousness seems to coincide with the beginning of a process of reversal of all values and all contents. In *Le bourgeois gentilhomme*, the opposition between good taste and bad taste is also an opposition between honesty and immorality, between passion and indifference; toward the end of the eighteenth century, people start considering aesthetic taste a sort of antidote to the Tree of Knowledge, after the experience of which the distinction between good and evil becomes impossible. And since the gates of the Garden of Eden are locked forever, the aesthete's voyage beyond good and evil inevitably ends with a diabolical temptation. In other words, the idea that there is a secret kinship between evil and the experience of art gains currency, and with it the position that in order to understand a work of art, open-mindedness and *Witz* are much more useful instruments than a good conscience. "He who does not scorn," says a character in Schlegel's *Lucinde*, "cannot appreciate, either. . . . So is not a certain *aesthetic cruelty* [*ästhetische Bösheit*] an essential part of harmonious education?"[13]

On the verge of the French Revolution, this peculiar perversion of the man of taste was taken to the extreme by Diderot in a short satire that, having already been translated into German by Goethe at the manuscript stage, exerted a powerful influence on young Hegel. In the satire, Rameau's nephew is a man of extraordinary good taste and at the same time a despicable rascal. In him every difference between good and evil, nobility and commonness, virtue and vice, has disappeared: only taste, in the middle of the absolute perversion of everything into its opposite, has maintained its integrity and lucidity. When Diderot asks him, "how is it that with a discrimination as delicate as yours and your remarkable sensitiveness for the beauties of musical art, you are so blind to the fine things of morality, so insensitive to the charms of virtue," Rameau's nephew replies that it is "apparently because some things need a sense I don't possess, a fibre that hasn't been vouchsafed me, or a slack one that you can tweak as much as you like but it won't vibrate."[14] In Rameau's nephew, that is, taste has worked like a sort of moral gangrene, devouring every other content and every other spiritual determination, and it exerts itself, in the end, in a total void. Taste is his only self-certainty and self-consciousness; however, this certainty is pure nothingness, and his personality is absolute impersonality. The very existence of such a man is a paradox and a scandal: he is incapable of producing a work of art, yet it is upon art that his existence depends; though condemned to depend on something other than himself, in this *other* he does not find any sense of what is essential, because every content and every moral determination is abolished. When Diderot asks him why he has not been able to produce anything worthwhile in spite of his gift for hearing, remembering, and reproducing, Rameau's nephew justifies himself by invoking the fatality that has endowed him with the ability to judge but not the ability to create, and recalls the legend of the statue of Memnon: "Round the statue of Memnon there were a multitude of other statues on which the sun's rays shone just the same, but Memnon's was the only one that gave forth a sound . . . the others . . . are just so many pairs of ears stuck on the end of so many poles."[15] The problem that finds its full and tragic self-consciousness in Rameau's nephew is that of the split between genius and taste, between artist and spectator, which, from this moment on, will dominate in an increasingly overt way the development of Western art. In Rameau's nephew, the spectator understands that he is an uncanny enigma: his justification, in an extreme form, is reminiscent of the experience of any sensitive person who, in front of a work of art he admires, almost feels defrauded and cannot suppress his wish that he had been its author. He is in front of something that, as it seems to him, puts him back in contact with his innermost truth, yet he cannot identify with it, since, as Kant said, the work of art is precisely "that which, even after one has achieved perfect knowledge of it, one is nonetheless still unable to produce." The spectator's is the most radical split: his principle is what is most alien to him; his essence is in that which, by definition, does not belong to him. Taste, in order fully to be, has to become separate from the principle of creation; but without genius, taste becomes a pure reversal, that is, *the very principle of perversion.*

Hegel was so strongly affected by the *Neveu de Rameau* that one could say that an entire section of the *Phenomenology of Spirit*, the one titled "Self-alienated spirit. Culture," is in fact nothing other than a comment on and an interpretation of this figure. In Rameau's nephew, Hegel saw the summit—and at the same time the beginning of the undoing—of European culture on the brink of the Terror and of the Revolution, when Spirit, having alienated itself in culture, can only find itself again in the consciousness of a split and in the absolute perversion of all concepts and all realities. Hegel called this concept "pure culture" and characterized it in these terms:

> When the pure "I" beholds itself outside of itself and split [*zerrissen*], then everything that has continuity and universality, everything that is called law, good, and right, is at the same time rent asunder and is destroyed. All identity dissolves away, for the utmost disparity now occupies the scene; what is absolutely essential is now absolutely unessential, being-for-self is now external to itself: the pure "I" itself is absolutely dismembered [*zersetzt*]. . . .
>
> Since, then, the condition of this consciousness is linked with this absolute split [*Zerrissenheit*], the distinction within its spirit of being noble, as opposed to ignoble, falls away and both are the same. . . .
>
> This self-consciousness which rebels against this rejection of itself is *eo ipso* absolutely self-identical in its absolute split, the pure mediation of pure self-consciousness with itself. It is the sameness of the identical judgment in which one and the same personality is both sub-

ject and predicate. But this identical judgment is at the same time the infinite judgment; for this personality is absolutely torn asunder, and subject and predicate are utterly indifferent, immediate beings which have nothing to do with one another, which have no necessary unity, so much so that each is the power of a separate independent personality. The being-for-self [of this consciousness, A.V.M.] has its own being-for-self for object as an out-and-out "other," and yet, at the same time, directly as its own self—itself as an "other"; not as if this had a different content, for the content is the same self in the form of an absolute antithesis and a completely indifferent existence of its own. Here, then, we have the Spirit of this real world of culture, Spirit that is *conscious* of itself in its truth and in its Notion.

It is this absolute and universal perversion [*Verkehrung*] and alienation of the actual world and of thought; it is *pure culture*. What is learnt in this world is that neither the *actuality* of power and wealth, nor their specific *Notions*, "good" and "bad," or the consciousness of "good" and "bad" (the noble and the ignoble consciousness), possess truth; on the contrary, all these moments become inverted, one changing into the other, and each is the opposite of itself. . . . The *thoughts* of these two essences, of "good" and "bad," are similarly inverted in this movement; what is characterized as good is bad, and vice versa. The consciousness of each of these moments, the consciousness judged as noble and ignoble, are rather in their truth just as much the reverse of what these characterizations are supposed to be; the noble consciousness is ignoble and repudiated, just as the repudiated consciousness changes round into the nobility which characterizes the most highly developed freedom of self-consciousness. From a formal standpoint, everything is *outwardly* the reverse of what it is *for itself*; and, again, it is not in truth what it is for itself, but something else than it wants to be; being-for-itself is rather the loss of itself, and its self-alienation rather the preservation of itself. What we have here, then, is that all the moments execute a universal justice on one another, each just as much alienates its own self, as it forms itself into its opposite and in this way inverts it.[16]

In front of Rameau's nephew, who has become conscious of the split in himself, the honest consciousness (the philosopher, in Diderot's dialogue) cannot say anything that the cowardly consciousness does not already know and say itself, because the latter is pre-

cisely the absolute perversion of everything into its opposite, and
its language is the judgment that, while it dissolves every identity,
plays this game of self-dissolution with itself as well. The only way
it has to reach self-possession is wholly to appropriate its contradiction and, negating itself, find itself again only in its extreme
split. However, precisely because he knows what is substantial only
under the guise of duality and alienation, Rameau's nephew on the
one hand is capable of *judging* it (and his language is in fact bril-
liant with intelligence) but on the other hand has lost the ability
to *grasp* it: his consciousness is radical inconsistency, his fullness is
absolute lack.

In characterizing culture as perversion, Hegel was aware that he
was describing a prerevolutionary state. In fact, his target was
French society at the point at which the values of the *ancien régime*
started wavering under the negating impulse of the Enlightenment:
in the *Phenomenology of Spirit*, the section devoted to absolute freedom and to the Terror follows closely upon the analysis of absolute
culture. The dialectic of honest and cowardly consciousness—each
of which is, in its essence, the opposite of itself, so that the first is
permanently destined to succumb to the second's frankness—is,
from this point of view, just as significant as the dialectic of master
and slave; but what is interesting to us here is that Hegel, wanting
to personify the absolute power of perversion, chose a figure such
as Rameau's nephew, as though the purest form of the man of taste,
for whom art is the only form of self-certainty as well as the most
painful split, would necessarily accompany the dissolution of social values and religious faith. And it is certainly not a simple co-
incidence if, when this dialectic reappears in European literature—
the first time in Dostoevsky's *Devils* with the old liberal intellectual
Stepan Stepanovich and, paired with him, his son Pjotr, and the
second time with the pair Settembrini-Naphta in Thomas Mann's
Magic Mountain—in both cases the experience that is described is
that of the undoing of a social microcosm in the face of the action
of Nietzsche's "uncanniest of all guests," European nihilism, per-
sonified by two mediocre but irresistible descendants of Rameau's
nephew.

The examination of aesthetic taste, then, leads us to ask whether there might not be a link of some kind between the destiny of art and the rise of that nihilism which, according to Heidegger's formulation, is in no way a historical movement like any other, but which, "thought in its essence, is . . . the fundamental movement of the history of the West."[17]

§ 4 The Cabinet of Wonder

In 1660, in Antwerp, David Teniers published the first illustrated catalog of an art museum under the title *Theatrum pittoricum.* In a series of etchings, the book reproduces the paintings owned by the archduke Leopold William and hung in his exhibition halls in the Brussels court. The author, addressing the "admirers of art" in his preface, warns that

> the original paintings whose drawings you see here are not all of the same shape or of the same size. Thus we have had to make them the same, in order to reduce them to the size of the pages of this volume, so that we could present them to you in a more convenient form. If somebody should wish to know the proportion of the originals, he can measure it guiding himself with the feet or palms which are marked in the margins.[1]

This warning is followed by a description of the halls themselves that could be a prototype of the guide found at the entrance of any modern museum, if it were not for the scant attention that Teniers pays the individual paintings rather than to the exhibition space as a whole:

> Upon entering, one encounters two long galleries, where, along the windowless wall, the Paintings hang in good order; on the other side, where the windows are, one can admire several large Statues, for the most part ancient ones, set on high Bases, with their ornaments; be-

hind them, under and between the windows, are other paintings, several of which you do not know.

Teniers informs us that among these are found six canvases by Bruegel the Elder, representing the twelve months of the year "with an admirable art of the brush, vivid colors, and ingenious ordering of postures," and a large number of still lives; from there one moves into other halls and exhibition areas "where the rarest and most precious rooms show the most subtle masterpieces of the brush, to the wonderful delight of the discerning Minds; so that the people who wish to look at such lovely things to their hearts' desire would need several weeks of leisure, or even many months, to examine them as closely as they deserve."

Art collections, however, have not always had such a familiar aspect for us. Toward the end of the Middle Ages, in the countries of continental Europe, princes and learned men used to collect the most disparate objects in a *Wunderkammer* (cabinet of wonder), which contained, promiscuously, rocks of an unusual shape, coins, stuffed animals, manuscript volumes, ostrich eggs, and unicorn horns. Statues and paintings stood side by side with curios and exemplars of natural history in these cabinets of wonders when people started collecting art objects; and, at least in Germanic countries, the princes' art collections preserved the traces of their origin in the medieval *Wunderkammer* until much later. We know that August I, elector of Saxony, who boasted that he owned "a series of portraits of Roman emperors, from Caesar to Domitian, executed by Titian from life," refused an offer of 100,000 gold florins made by Venice's Council of the Ten for a unicorn he owned, and that he kept as a precious object a stuffed phoenix, a gift from the bishop of Bamberg. As late as 1567, the exhibition room kept by Albert V of Bavaria contained, in addition to 780 paintings, 2,000 objects of various kinds, among them "an egg that a bishop had found inside another egg, manna fallen from the sky during a famine, a hydra, and a basilisk."

We have an etching that reproduces the *Wunderkammer* belonging to the German physician and collector Hans Worms, with the help of which we can gain a fairly precise notion of the appearance of a real cabinet of wonder. Alligators, stuffed gray bears, oddly shaped fish, stuffed birds, and canoes used by primitive peoples hang from the ceiling, at a considerable distance from the floor. The upper part of the back wall is taken up by spears, arrows, and other weapons of various shapes and origins. Between the windows of one of the side walls there are deer and elk antlers, animal hooves and skulls; on the opposite wall, in near proximity to each other, hang tortoise shells, snake skins, sawfish teeth, and leopard skins. From a certain height all the way down to the floor, the walls are covered with shelves overflowing with shells, octopus bones, mineral salts, metals, roots, and mythological statuettes. Only seemingly does chaos reign in the *Wunderkammer*, however: to the mind of the medieval scholar, it was a sort of microcosm that reproduced, in its harmonious confusion, the animal, vegetable, and mineral macrocosm. This is why the individual objects seem to find their meaning only side by side with others, between the walls of a room in which the scholar could measure at every moment the boundaries of the universe.

If we now lift our eyes away from the etching and turn them to a painting that reproduces a seventeenth-century gallery, for example the picture by Willem van Haecht that depicts the archduke Albert visiting Cornelius van der Geist's collection in Antwerp, in the company of Rubens, Gerard Seghers, and Jordaens, we cannot help noticing a certain similarity. The walls are literally covered, from the floor to the ceiling, with paintings of the most diverse sizes and materials, almost touching each other so as to form a pictorial magma that recalls Frenhofer's "wall of paint" and in which the single work would have had little chance of being noticed. Next to a door, in equal confusion, stands a group of statues, among which we can make out only with difficulty an Apollo, a Venus, a Bacchus, and a Diana. The dense group of artists and gentlemen gathered around a low table covered with small sculptures stands out among the other paintings that are piled up all over the floor. On the lintel of one of the doors, under a coat of arms above which is a skull, is an easily legible inscription: *Vive l'Esprit* (long live intelligence).

It has been observed that we feel as though we were not in front of paintings but in front of one immense tapestry in which vague colors and shapes fluctuate, and the question comes naturally whether the same thing may not apply to these paintings as to the medieval scholar's shells and whale teeth: namely, that they acquired their truth and their authentic meaning only through their inclusion in the harmonic microcosm of the *Wunderkammer*. It seems, that is, that the single canvases have no reality outside the unmoving *Theatrum pittoricum* to which they are consigned, or at least that they acquire all their enigmatic meaning only in this ideal space. But while the microcosm of the *Wunderkammer* had its profound reason in its living and immediate unity with the great world of divine creation, it would be vain to seek an analogous foundation for the gallery: enclosed by the vivid colors of its walls, it rests in itself like a perfectly self-sufficient world where the canvases resemble the sleeping princess of the fairy tale, prisoner of a spell whose magic formula is inscribed on the door's lintel: *Vive l'Esprit*.

In the same year in which, in Antwerp, Teniers published his *Theatrum pittoricum*, Marco Boschini's *Carta del navegar pittoresco* (Chart of pictorial navigation) also appeared. This book interests the art historian because of the multifarious information on seventeenth-century Venetian painting it provides us with and for the embryonic aesthetic judgments on individual painters that it sketches; but it is particularly interesting for us because, after leading the "Venetian Ship" across "the high seas of Painting," Boschini concludes his adventurous itinerary with the meticulous description of an imaginary gallery. Boschini lingers for a long time on the shape that, according to the taste of the time, the walls and the corners of the ceilings must have:

> L'opera su i sofiti, che xé piani
> e' i fenze in archi, e in volti li trasforma.
> Cusì de piani ai concavi el dà forma
> e tesse a i ochi industriosi ingani.
>
> El fa che i cantonali in forma acuta
> salta fuora con angoli spicanti,
> e in pe' de andare in drento, i vien avanti.
> Questo è loquace, e no' pitura muta.

(The work on the ceilings, which are flat,
molds them into arches, and transforms them into vaults.
Thus he gives to concave spaces the look of flat ones
and weaves ingenious deceptions for the eyes.

He makes it so that the corner cupboards, in acute shape,
jump out with outstanding angles,
and instead of going in, come forward.
This is loquacious, and not mute painting.)[2]

He does not even neglect to specify, for every room, the color and kind of wall coverings for this purely mental décor.

Although architectural rules for the construction of galleries had already been put in writing, this is one of the first times that these precepts, instead of being contained in an architectural treatise, are given as the ideal conclusion to what we could define as a vast critical-descriptive treatise on painting. It seems that for Boschini, his imaginary gallery is in some way the most concrete space of painting, a sort of ideal connecting fabric that is able to ensure a unitary foundation to the disparate creations of the artists' genius, as though, once abandoned to the stormy sea of painting, they could reach dry land only on the perfectly set up scene of this virtual theater. Boschini is so convinced of this that he even compares the paintings sleeping in the halls of the gallery to balms, which, in order to acquire their full power, have to rest in their glass containers:

Balsamo è la Pitura precioso,
per l'intelletto vera medesina,
che più che 'l sta in te 'l vaso, el se rafina,
e in cao cent'anni lé miracoloso.

(Painting is a precious balm,
true medicine for the intellect,
and the more it stays in its vial the more refined it gets,
and by a hundred years later it is miraculous.)

Although we do not make use of such ingenuous images, it is probable that our aesthetic perspective on art, which makes us build museums and makes it appear normal to us that the painting should go immediately from the hands of the artist to a hall in the museum of contemporary art, is based on not too dissimilar assumptions. What is certain, at any rate, is that the work of art is no longer, at this point, the essential measure of man's dwelling on earth, which, precisely because it builds and makes possible the act of dwelling, has neither an autonomous sphere nor a particular identity, but is a compendium and reflection of the entire human world. On the contrary, art has now built its own world for itself. Consigned to the atemporal aesthetic dimension of the *Museum Theatrum*, it begins its second and interminable life, which, while it will keep increasing its metaphysical and monetary value, will also eventually dissolve the concrete space of the work until the latter resembles the convex mirror that Boschini wished to hang on a wall of his imaginary gallery,

> dove l'ogeto, in pe' de farse appresso
> e se fa un passo in drio, per so' avantazo.

> (where the object, instead of coming closer,
> steps backward, to its advantage.)

We believe, then, that we have finally secured for art its most authentic reality, but when we try to grasp it, it draws back and leaves us empty-handed.

～

However, the work of art was not always considered a collector's object. There have been epochs when the very idea of art as we conceive it would have appeared monstrous. Love of art for its own sake is almost never encountered in the Middle Ages, and when its first symptoms appeared, mixed up with the taste for pomp and precious objects, the common view considered them aberrations.

In these epochs, the subjectivity of the artist was identified so immediately with his material—which constituted, not only for him but also for his fellow men, the innermost truth of consciousness—that it would have appeared inconceivable to speak about art as having value in itself, and in front of the finished work of art it was impossible to speak of aesthetic participation. In the four large sections (Mirror of Nature, Mirror of Science, Mirror of Morals, Mirror of History) of the *Speculum Majus*, in which Vincent of Beauvais lodged the entire universe, there is no room for art because it did not represent in any way, for the medieval mind, a realm of the universe among others. When the medieval man looked at the tympanum of the Vezelay cathedral, with its sculptures depicting all the peoples of the world in the single light of divine Pentecost, or the column in the Souvigny abbey, with its four sides reproducing the wonderful ends of the earth through the images of the fabulous inhabitants of those regions—the goat-legged Satyr, the Sciapodes who moves on one foot, the horse-hoofed Hippopode, the Ethiopian, the manticore, and the unicorn—he had the aesthetic impression not that he was observing a work of art but rather that he was measuring, more concretely for him, the borders of his world. The wonderful was not yet an autonomous sentimental tonality and the particular effect of the work of art, but an indistinct presence of the grace that, in the work, put man's activity in tune with the divine world of creation, and thus kept alive the echo of what art had been in its Greek beginnings: the wonderful and uncanny power of making being and the world appear, of *producing* them in the work. Johan Huizinga reports the case of Denis the Carthusian, who tells how once, upon entering the Church of Saint John at Bois-le-Duc while the organ was playing, he was immediately entranced by the melody and brought to a prolonged ecstasy: "Musical sensation was immediately absorbed in religious feeling. It would never have occurred to Denis that he might admire in music or painting any other beauty than that of holy things themselves."[3]

And yet, at some point we see the stuffed crocodile suspended at the entrance to St. Bertrand de Comminges and the unicorn foot that was kept in the sacristy of the Sainte Chapelle in Paris leave the sacred space of the cathedral to enter the collector's cabinet, and we also see the sensibility of the spectator in front of the work of art linger for so long on the instant of wonder as to isolate it as an autonomous sphere from any religious or moral content.

~

In the chapter of the *Lectures on Aesthetics* devoted to the dissolution of romantic art, Hegel felt all the importance of the living identity between the artist and his material and understood that the destiny of Western art could be explained only starting from a scission whose consequences we are now able to measure for the first time.

> So long as the artist is bound up with the specific character of such a world-view and religion, in immediate identity with it and with firm faith in it, so long is he genuinely in earnest with this material and its representation; i.e. this material remains for him the infinite and true element in his own consciousness—a material with which he lives in an original unity as part of his inmost self, while the form in which he exhibits it is for him as artist the final, necessary, and supreme manner of bringing before our contemplation the Absolute and the soul of objects in general. By the substance of his material, a substance immanent in himself, he is tied down to the specific mode of its exposition. For in that case the material, and therefore the form belonging to it, the artist carries immediately in himself as the proper essence of his existence which he does not imagine for himself but which he *is*; and therefore he only has the task of making this truly essential element objective to himself, to present and develop it in a living way out of his own resources.[4]

Yet, fatally, the moment will come when this immediate unity of the artist's subjectivity with his material breaks. The artist then experiences a radical tearing or split, by which the inert world of contents in their indifferent, prosaic objectivity goes to one side, and to the other the free subjectivity of the artistic principle, which soars above the contents as over an immense repository of materials that it can evoke or reject at will. Art is now the absolute freedom that seeks its end and its foundation in itself, and does not need, substantially, any content, because it can only measure itself against the vertigo caused by its own abyss. No longer is any other content—except art itself—*immediately* for the artist the substantiality of his consciousness, nor does it inspire him with the necessity of representing it:

Now contrasted with the time in which the artist owing to his nationality and his period stands with the substance of his being within a specific world-view and its content and forms of portrayal, we find an altogether opposed view which in its complete development is of importance only in most recent times. In our day, in the case of almost all peoples, criticism, the cultivation of reflection, and, in our German case, freedom of thought have mastered the artists too, and have made them, so to say, a *tabula rasa* in respect of the material and the form of their productions, after the necessary particular stages of the romantic art-form have been traversed. Bondage to a particular subject-matter and a mode of portrayal suitable for this material alone are for artists today something past, and art therefore has become a free instrument which the artist can wield in proportion to his subjective skill in relation to any material of whatever kind. The artist thus stands above specific consecrated forms and configurations and moves freely on his own account, independent of the subject-matter and mode of conception in which the holy and eternal was previously made visible to human apprehension. No content, no form, is any longer immediately identical with the inwardness, the nature, the unconscious substantial essence of the artist; every material may be indifferent to him if only it does not contradict the formal law of being simply beautiful and capable of artistic treatment. Today there is no material which stands in and for itself above this relativity, and even if one matter be raised above it, still there is at least no absolute need for its representation by *art*.[5]

This scission marks too decisive an event in the destiny of Western art for us to fancy that we can have a total view over the horizon that it unveils; however, we can already recognize, among its first consequences, the manifestation of that fracture between taste and genius that we saw emerging in the figure of the man of taste and attaining its most problematic formulation in the character of Rameau's nephew. So long as the artist lives in intimate unity with his material, the spectator sees in the work of art only his own faith and the highest truth of his being brought to art in the most necessary manner, and a problem of art as such cannot arise since art is precisely the shared space in which all men, artists and non-artists, come together in living unity. But once the creative subjectivity of the artist begins to place itself above his material and his production, like a playwright who freely puts his characters on the scene, this shared concrete space of the work of art dissolves, and what the spectator sees in it is no longer something that he can immediately find again in his consciousness as his highest truth. Everything that the spectator can still find in the work of art is, now, mediated by aesthetic representation, which is itself, independently of any content, the supreme value and the most intimate truth that unfolds its power in the artwork itself and starting from the artwork itself. The free creative principle of the artist rises up like a precious veil of Maya between the spectator and such truth as he can attain in the work of art, a veil of which he will never be able to take possession concretely, but only through the reflection in the magic mirror of his taste.

If the spectator recognizes in this absolute principle the highest truth of his being in the world, he must coherently think his reality starting from the eclipse of all content and of all moral and religious determination; like Rameau's nephew, he condemns himself to seeking his substance in what is most alien to him. Thus the birth of taste coincides with the absolute split of "pure Culture": the spectator sees himself as other in the work of art, his being-for-himself as being-outside-himself; and in the pure creative subjectivity at work in the work of art, he does not in any way recover a determinate content and a concrete measure of his existence, but recovers simply his own self in the form of absolute alienation, and he can possess himself only inside this split.

The original unity of the work of art has broken, leaving on the one side the aesthetic judgment and on the other artistic subjectivity without content, the pure creative principle. Both vainly seek their grounding, and in this search they incessantly dissolve the concreteness of the work, the one by bringing it back to the ideal space of the *Museum Theatrum*, the other by transcending it in its constant movement beyond itself. For just as the spectator, faced with the alienness of the creative principle, attempts to place his foundation in the Museum, where the absolute split reverses into absolute sameness with himself "in the identity of the judgment in which the same personality is both subject and predicate," so the artist—who has made in his creation the demiurgic experience of absolute freedom—strives for the objectivization of his world and for self-possession. At the end of this process we find Baudelaire's sentence: "la poésie est ce qu'il y a de plus réel, ce qui n'est complètement vrai que dans un autre monde" ("poetry is what is most real, what is completely true only in another world"). In front of the aesthetic-metaphysical space of the gallery, another space opens up that corresponds to it metaphysically: the purely mental space of Frenhofer's canvas, in which artistic subjectivity without content, through a kind of alchemical operation, actualizes its impossible truth. To the *Museum Theatrum* as *topos ouranios* of art in the perspective of aesthetic judgment corresponds the "other world" of poetry, the *Theatrum chemicum* as *topos ouranios* of the absolute artistic principle.

Lautréamont is the artist who lived this splitting up and redoubling of art to its most paradoxical consequences. Rimbaud had gone from the hell of poetry to the hell of Harar, from words to silence: by contrast, the more naive Lautréamont abandons the Promethean cave that had seen the birth of the *Songs of Maldoror* for the high-school classroom or the university lecture hall where the elegant *poncifs* (clichés) of his *Poésies* will have to be declaimed. The poet who had taken to its extreme consequences the need for absolute artistic subjectivity and had seen the limits of the human and the inhuman become blurred in this attempt now takes to its extreme consequences the perspective of aesthetic judgment, to the point of stating that "les chefs-d'oeuvre de la langue française sont les discours de distribution pour les lycées et les discours académiques" ("the masterpieces of the French language are the speeches for school award ceremonies and academic speeches") and that "les jugements sur la poésie ont plus de valeur que la poésie" ("judgments on poetry are worth more than poetry"). The fact that he was only able to oscillate between the two extremes of this movement without however being able to recover their unity demonstrates merely that the abyss in which our aesthetic conception of art is founded cannot be so easily filled, and that the two metaphysical realities of the aesthetic judgment and of artistic subjectivity without content incessantly refer back and forth to each other.

But in the reciprocal support given by the two "other worlds" of art, precisely the only two questions that our meditation on art should answer in order to be consistent with itself remain unanswered: *What is the foundation of the aesthetic judgment? And what is the foundation of artistic subjectivity without content?*

§ 5 "Les jugements sur la poésie
ont plus de valeur que la poésie"

"Judgments on poetry are worth more than poetry." We do not yet think seriously enough about the meaning of aesthetic judgment: how could we take Lautréamont's sentence seriously? And we will not be able to reflect upon this sentence in its proper dimension so long as we see in it simply a play of reversal, performed in the name of an incomprehensible mockery, and until we ask ourselves instead whether its truth may not perhaps be sculpted into the very structure of modern sensibility.

We are approaching its secret meaning when we relate it to what Hegel writes in his introduction to the *Lectures on Aesthetics*, when he asks about the destiny of art in his time. Then, to our surprise, we notice that the conclusions reached by Hegel not only are not very far from Lautréamont's but in fact allow the latter to sound far less paradoxical to us than they have up to now.

Hegel observes that the work of art does not satisfy the soul's spiritual needs as it did in earlier times, because our tendency toward reflection and toward a critical stance have become so strong that when we are before a work of art we no longer attempt to penetrate its innermost vitality, identifying ourselves with it, but rather attempt to represent it to ourselves according to the critical framework furnished by the aesthetic judgment.

What is now aroused in us by works of art is not just our immediate enjoyment but our judgement also, since we subject to our intellectual consideration (i) the content of art, and (ii) the work of art's means of presentation, and the appropriateness or inappropriateness of both to one another. The *philosophy* of art is therefore a greater need in our day than it was in days when art by itself as art yielded full satisfaction. Art invites us to intellectual consideration, and that not for the purpose of creating art again, but for knowing philosophically what art is. . . . Art . . . acquires its real ratification only in philosophy.[1]

The times are long past in which Denis the Carthusian was entranced by the melody of the organ in the Church of Saint John at Bois-le-Duc; the work of art is no longer, for modern man, the concrete appearance of the divine, which causes either ecstasy or sacred terror in the soul, but a privileged occasion to exercise his critical taste, that judgment on art which, if it is not actually worth more than art itself for us, certainly addresses a need that is at least as essential.

This has become such a spontaneous and familiar experience for us that it does not even occur to us to ask ourselves about the mechanism of aesthetic judgment every time that, in front of a work of art, we worry first of all, almost unconsciously, about whether it is in fact art and not false art, non-art, and that we subject to our meditation, as Hegel said, the content, the means of its manifestation, and the appropriateness of both. In fact, it is likely that this mysterious kind of conditioned reflex, with its question about being and nonbeing, is simply one aspect of a much more general attitude that Western man, ever since his Greek beginnings, has almost always had before the world around him, asking every time τι το ὄν, what is this thing that is, and distinguishing the ὄν, that which is, from the μὴ ὄν, that which is not.

If we now linger a few moments on the most coherent meditation on aesthetic judgment that the Western world has, Kant's *Critique of Judgment*, what surprises us is not so much that the problem of the beautiful is presented only from the point of view of the aesthetic judgment—this is, in fact, perfectly natural—but that the judgment identifies the determinations of beauty only in a purely negative fashion. As is well known, Kant, following the blueprint of the transcendental analytic, defines the beautiful in four moments, determining in succession the four essential characteristics of aesthetic judgment. According to the first definition, "*taste* is the faculty of judging of an object or a method of representing it by an *entirely disinterested* satisfaction or dissatisfaction. The object of such satisfaction is called beautiful."[2] The second definition specifies that "the beautiful is that which apart from concepts is represented as the object of a universal satisfaction"(§ 6, p. 45). The third is that "*beauty* is the form of the *purposiveness* of an object, so far as this is perceived in it *without any representation of a purpose*" (§ 17, p. 73). Finally, the fourth adds that "the *beautiful* is that which without any concept is cognized as the object of a universal satisfaction" (§ 22, p. 77).

Faced with these four characteristics of beauty as the object of aesthetic judgment (namely, disinterested satisfaction, universality apart from concepts, purposiveness without purpose, and normality without a norm), one cannot help but think of what Nietzsche wrote in his polemic against the long error of metaphysics in *The Twilight of the Idols*: "the distinctive marks that have been considered the real essence of things are the distinctive marks of non-being, *of nothingness.*" It seems, that is, that every time aesthetic judgment attempts to determine what the beautiful is, it holds in its hands not the beautiful but its shadow, as though its true object were not so much what art is but what it is not: not art but non-art.

If we just begin to observe the functioning of the mechanism of critical judgment in us, we must admit, even against ourselves, that everything our critical judgment suggests to us before a work of art belongs precisely to this shadow. In the act of judgment that separates art from non-art, we turn non-art into the content of art, and it is only in this negative mold that we are able to rediscover its reality. When we deny that a work is artistic, we mean that it has all the material elements of a work of art with the exception of something essential on which its life depends, just in the same way that we say that a corpse has all the elements of the living body, except that ungraspable *something* that makes of it a living being. Yet, when we actually find ourselves before a work of art, we behave unconsciously like a medical student who has studied anatomy only on corpses and who, faced with the pulsing organs of the patient, must mentally refer back to his dead anatomical model in order to orient himself.

Whatever criterion the critical judgment employs to measure the reality of the work—its linguistic structure, its historical dimension, the authenticity of the *Erlebnis* from which it has sprung, and so on—it will only have laid out, in place of a living body, an interminable skeleton of dead elements, and the work of art will have actually become for us, as Hegel says, the beautiful fruit picked from the tree that a friendly Fate has placed before us, without, however, giving back to us, together with it, either the branch that has borne it or the soil that has nourished it or the changing seasons that have helped it ripen.[3] What has been negated is reassumed into the judgment as its only real content, and what has been affirmed is covered by this shadow. Our appreciation of art begins necessarily with the forgetting of art.

Thus, aesthetic judgment confronts us with the embarrassing paradox of an instrument that is indispensable to us in knowing the work of art, but that not only does not allow us to penetrate its reality but also at the same time points us toward something other than art and represents art's reality to us as pure and simple nothingness. Like a complex and articulate negative theology, criticism everywhere attempts to circumvent something that cannot be encompassed by wrapping itself up in the latter's shadow, in a process reminiscent of the Veda's "not this, not this" and Saint Bernard's "I do not know, I do not know." Caught up in laboriously constructing this nothingness, we do not notice that in the meantime art has become a planet of which we only see the dark side, and that aesthetic judgment is then nothing other than the *logos*, the reunion of art and its shadow.

If we wanted to express this characteristic with a formula, we could write that critical judgment thinks art as ~~art~~, meaning by this that the critical judgment, everywhere and consistently, envelops art in its shadow and thinks art as non-art. It is this ~~art~~, that is, a pure shadow, that reigns as a supreme value over the horizon of *terra aesthetica,* and it is likely that we will not be able to get beyond this horizon until we have inquired about the foundation of aesthetic judgment.

~

The enigma of this foundation remains concealed in the origin and the destiny of modern thought. Ever since Kant's failed attempt to find a satisfactory answer to the only question that actually counts in the history of aesthetics—namely, "how are *a priori* aesthetic judgments possible, with respect to their foundation?"—this original blemish is a burden on us every time we utter a judgment about art.

Kant asked about the foundation of aesthetic judgment in terms of the quest for a solution to the antinomy of taste, which he summarized as follows in the second section of the *Critique of Judgment*:

> *Thesis*: The judgment of taste is not based upon concepts, for otherwise it would admit of controversy (would be determinable by proofs).
> *Antithesis*: The judgment of taste is based on concepts, for otherwise, despite its diversity, we could not quarrel about it (we could not claim for our judgment the necessary assent of others). (§ 56, pp. 183–84)

Kant attempted to solve this antinomy by putting at the basis of aesthetic judgment something that had the characteristics of a concept, but which was in no way determinable and thus could not provide the proof for the judgment itself: "a concept . . . from which . . . nothing can be known."

> But all contradiction disappears if I say: the judgment of taste is based on a concept (viz. the concept of the general ground of the subjective purposiveness of nature for the judgment) from which, however, nothing can be known and proved in respect of the object, because it is in itself indeterminable and useless for knowledge. Yet at the same time and on that very account the judgment has validity for everyone (though, of course, for each only as a singular judgment immediately accompanying his intuition), because its determining ground lies per-

haps in the concept of that which may be regarded as the supersensible substrate of humanity. . . . The subjective principle, viz. the indefinite idea of the supersensible in us, can only be put forward as the sole key to the puzzle of this faculty whose sources are hidden from us; it can be made no further intelligible. (§ 57, pp. 186–87)

Kant probably recognized that this founding of aesthetic judgment through an indefinite idea resembled a mystical intuition more than a solid rational foundation, and that the "sources" of judgment thus remained shrouded in the most impenetrable mystery. However, he also knew that once art was conceived in an aesthetic dimension, there was no other way to put reason in accord with itself. He had unconsciously perceived the split inherent in judgment of artistic beauty when he compared it with judgment of natural beauty. This comparison convinced him that while the latter does not require that we already have a concept of what the object should be, we do need such a concept when we judge artistic beauty, because the foundation of the work of art is something other than us, namely, the free creative-formal principle of the artist. This led him to oppose taste, the judging faculty, to genius, the productive faculty, and in order to reconcile the radical otherness of the two principles, he had to resort to the mystical idea of the supersensible substratum that founds both.

Thus the problem of Rameau's nephew, the scission of taste and genius, continues to exercise a secret dominion over the problem of the origin of aesthetic judgment. Benedetto Croce wanted to solve this problem by identifying aesthetic judgment with aesthetic production and writing that "the difference [between genius and taste] consists only in the difference in circumstances, since in the one case there is aesthetic production and in the other case aesthetic reproduction,"[4] as though the enigma were not precisely this "difference in circumstances." The unforgivable carelessness of this solution testifies to how deeply that variance is inscribed in the destiny of modernity and shows how aesthetic judgment necessarily begins by forgetting its own origin.

Within the horizon of our aesthetic apprehension, the work of art remains subject to a kind of law of the degradation of energy:

one can never return to it from a state posterior to its creation. Just as a physical system that is isolated from the outside can go from state A to state B but can never again return to its original state, so once the work of art has been produced, there is no way to return to it by way of the reverse path of taste. Aesthetic judgment, much as it tries to repair the split that inhabits it, cannot escape this law, which we might call the law of the degradation of artistic energy. And if one day criticism should undergo a trial, the accusation against which it would be least able to defend itself would be precisely that it has adopted an insufficiently self-critical stance, neglecting to ask about its own origin and its own meaning.

However, as has been said, history is not a bus you can get off of, and so, despite this original fault, and however contradictory we might find this, in the meantime aesthetic judgment has become the essential organ of our sensibility before the work of art. It has become that to such an extent that out of the ashes of Rhetoric it has allowed a science to be born for which, in its present structure, there is no equivalent in any other time. Moreover, it has created a figure, that of the modern critic, whose only reason for being and exclusive task is the exercise of aesthetic judgment.

This figure bears within its activity the obscure contradictoriness of its origin. Wherever the critic encounters art, he brings it back to its opposite, dissolving it in non-art; wherever he exercises his reflection, he brings with him nonbeing and shadow, as though he had no other means to worship art than the celebration of a kind of black mass in honor of the *deus inversus*, the inverted god, of non-art. If one browses through the enormous mass of the writings by the *lundistes* of the nineteenth century, from the most obscure to the most famous, one is surprised to notice that they reserve the most consideration and the most space not to the good artists but to mediocre and bad ones. Proust was ashamed to read what Sainte-Beuve wrote of Baudelaire and Balzac, and observed that if all the works of the nineteenth century except the *Lundis* were burned, and if therefore we had to base only on them our opinion of the relative importance of writers, we would think that Stendhal and Flaubert must be much inferior to Charles de Bernard,

Vinet, Molé, Ramond, and other third-rate writers.[5] The entire century that defined itself ("no doubt by antiphrasis," Jean Paulhan wrote ironically) as the century of criticism seems dominated from end to end by the principle that the good critic must go wrong on the good writer: Villemain engaged in polemics with Chateaubriand; Brunetière denied the value of Stendhal and Flaubert; Lemaitre did the same to Verlaine and Mallarmé; Faguet, the same to Nerval and Zola; and, to come to times closer to us, let us only recall the summary judgment with which Croce disposed of Rimbaud and Mallarmé.

And yet, if we look closer, this apparently fatal error reveals itself instead as the only means available to the critic to remain faithful to his task and to his original fault. If he did not continually bring art back to its shadow—if, by distinguishing art from non-art, he did not each time make of the latter the content of the former and thus risk confusing them, our aesthetic idea of art would lose all consistency. Gone is the time when the artist was bound, in immediate identity, to faith and to the conceptions of his world; no longer is the work of art founded in the unity of the artist's subjectivity with the work's content in such a way that the spectator may immediately find in it the highest truth of his consciousness, that is, the divine.

As we saw in the previous chapter, the supreme truth of the work of art is now the pure creative-formal principle that fulfills its potentiality in it, independently of any content. This means that what is essential for the spectator in the work of art is precisely what is alien to him and deprived of essence, while what he sees of himself in the work, that is, the content he perceives, appears to him no longer as a truth that finds its necessary expression in the work, but rather as something of which he is already perfectly aware as a thinking subject, and which therefore he can legitimately believe himself capable of expressing. Thus the condition of a Raphael without hands is in a certain sense the normal spiritual condition of any spectator who actually cares for the work of art, and the experience of art can only be the experience of an absolute split. As Hegel understood, modeling on Rameau's nephew his dialectic of

the split, "the identical judgement in which one and the same personality is both subject and predicate" is at the same time necessarily "an infinite judgement; for this personality is absolutely di-
rempted [*entzweit*] and subject and predicate are utterly indifferent entities which have nothing to do with one another."[6]

In the aesthetic judgment, being-for-itself has as its object its
own being-for-itself, but as something absolutely Other, and at the
same time immediately as itself; it is the pure split and lack of
foundation that endlessly drifts on the ocean of form without ever
reaching dry land.

If the spectator consents to the radical alienation of this experience, leaves behind all content and all support, and agrees to enter
the circle of absolute perversion, he has no other way of finding
himself again than wholly to assume his contradiction. That is, he
must split asunder his own split, negate his own negation, suppress
his own being suppressed; he is the absolute will to be other and
the movement that simultaneously divides the violin from and
unites it with the piece of wood that has found itself to be a violin, divides the bugle from and unites it with the copper that has
woken up as a bugle.[7] In this alienation he owns himself, and in
owning himself he alienates himself.

The space that supports the museum is this incessant and absolute negation of oneself and the other, in which the split is reconciled for an instant and the spectator, negating himself, accepts
himself, only to become immersed, in the next moment, in a new
negation. In this uncanny abyss our aesthetic apprehension of art
finds its foundation: its positive value in our society and its metaphysical consistency in the sky of aesthetics rest on the work of
negating this nothingness that laboriously goes around its annihilation. Only in this step backward that we force it to take toward
its shadow does the work of art reacquire for us a familiar dimension that can be an object of rational inquiry.

If, then, it is true that the critic leads art to its negation, it is only
in this shadow and this death that art (our aesthetic idea of art) sustains itself and finds its reality. Thus the critic ends up resembling
the Inquisitor in Ivan Karamazov's little poem, who, in order to

make possible a Christian world, has to negate Christ when he has him before his eyes.

◯

Today, however, it seems that this irritating yet irreplaceable instrument of our aesthetic apprehension of art is undergoing a crisis that could lead to its eclipse. In one of the "Unfriendly Observations" collected by Robert Musil in his *Nachlaß zu Lebzeiten* (Posthumous papers of a living author), Musil jokingly asked "whether kitsch, increased by one and then two dimensions of kitsch, would not become increasingly bearable and increasingly less kitsch," and, trying to discover the relationship between kitsch and art by means of a curious mathematical calculation, concluded that they appear to be the very same thing.[8] After aesthetic judgment taught us to distinguish art from its shadow and authenticity from inauthenticity, our experience, on the contrary, forces us to face the embarrassing truth that it is precisely to non-art that we owe, today, our most original aesthetic emotions. Who has not experienced at least once, faced with kitsch, a pleasant freeing sensation, affirming, against all suggestions of his critical sense: This object is aesthetically ugly, and yet I like it and I am touched by it? One could surmise that the whole vast area of the outside world and of our sensitivity that critical judgment had pushed back into the limbo of non-art has started to become conscious of its necessity and of its dialectical function, and that, in a rebellion against the tyranny of good taste, it has shown up to claim its rights.

However, another and far more extravagant phenomenon presents itself today for our consideration. While the work of art is intelligible to us only by way of the comparison with its shadow, in order to appreciate the beauty of natural objects, as Kant sensed, we have never needed to measure them against their negation. Thus it would certainly never have occurred to us to ask whether a storm was more or less successful or a flower more or less original, because our judgment did not perceive behind natural production the otherness of a formal principle, although this used to be a question that we spontaneously asked before a painting, a novel, or any other work of genius.

If we observe now what is offered by our experience, we notice that this relationship is in the process somehow of being reversed right under our noses. More and more frequently, contemporary art presents us with productions before which it is no longer possible to resort to the traditional mechanism of the aesthetic judgment, and for which the antagonistic polarity *art/non-art* appears totally inadequate. In front of a "ready-made," for instance, in which the otherness of the formal-creative principle has been replaced by the alienation of the non-artistic object that is inserted by force into the sphere of art, critical judgment is, so to speak, immediately confronted with itself, or to be more precise, with its image in reverse: what it is supposed to trace back to non-art is already non-art on its own, and the critic's operation is limited to an ID check. Contemporary art, in its most recent tendencies, has further advanced this process and has by now produced that "reciprocal ready-made" Duchamp was thinking of when he suggested the use of a Rembrandt painting as an ironing board. The extreme object-centeredness of contemporary art, through its holes, stains, slits, and nonpictorial materials, tends increasingly to identify the work of art with the non-artistic product. Thus, becoming aware of its shadow, art immediately receives in itself its own negation, and in bridging the gap that used to separate it from criticism, itself becomes the *logos* of art and of its shadow, that is, critical reflection on art, ~~art~~. In contemporary art, it is critical judgment that lays bare its own split, thus suppressing and rendering superfluous its own space.

At the same time, a contrary process is taking place in the way we think of nature. While we are no longer able to judge a work of art aesthetically, our intelligence of nature has grown so opaque, and, moreover, the presence in it of the human element has grown to such an extent, that sometimes, in front of a landscape, we spontaneously compare it to its shadow, wondering whether it is aesthetically beautiful or ugly, and we have ever more serious difficulties distinguishing from a work of art a mineral precipitate or a piece of wood that has been eroded and filed by the chemical action of time.

Thus we find it natural to speak today of "land conservancy" in the same way that we speak of the preservation of a work of art, both ideas that would have struck other eras as inconceivable. It is also likely that we will soon create institutes to restore natural beauty just like those for the restoration of works of art, without recognizing that such an idea presupposes a radical transformation of our relationship to nature, and that the inability to penetrate a landscape without spoiling it and the desire to purify it from such penetration are two sides of the same coin. What used to present itself to aesthetic judgment as absolute otherness has now become something familiar and natural, while natural beauty, which was, for our judgment, a familiar reality, has become something radically alien: art has become nature, and nature, art.

The first consequence of this reversal is that criticism has relinquished its proper function—namely, the exercise of that judgment that we have defined as the *logos* of art and of its shadow—and has become scientific research on art according to the schemes of information theory (which considers art to be precisely *on this side* of the distinction between art and non-art) or, in the best of cases, a search for the impossible meaning of art from a non-aesthetic perspective, which however always ends up relapsing into aesthetics.

Critical judgment, then, seems to be going through an eclipse, about whose duration and consequences we can only make guesses. One of these—and not the most pessimistic—is that if we do not start to ask right now, forcefully, about the foundation of critical judgment, the idea of art as we know it will slip through our fingers without a new idea to take its place effectively. Unless, that is, we resolve to extract from this temporary opaqueness the question capable of burning from head to toe the phoenix of aesthetic judgment and to allow a more original, that is, more initial, way to think art.

§ 6 A Self-Annihilating Nothing

So that nobody may accuse him of crudeness and insensitivity for banning poetry from his city, Plato informs us in the last book of the *Republic* that the divorce (διαφορά) between philosophy and poetry was already considered in his times something of an "old animosity." In order to prove this statement, he quotes several somewhat irreverent expressions that the poets had directed at philosophy, defining it as "the yelping hound barking at her master," "the band of philosophers who have made Zeus a slave," "mighty in the idle babble of fools," and so on.[1] We are so used to this divorce that we are unable to perceive to what decisive extent it dominates the destiny of Western culture. Yet, if we wanted to delineate its enigmatic history, it is likely that we would have to identify as the second fundamental event, after Plato's ban, Hegel's statement on art in the first part of his *Lectures on Aesthetics*:

> But while on the one hand we give this high position to art, it is on the other hand just as necessary to remember that neither in content nor in form is art the highest and absolute mode of bringing to our minds the true interests of the spirit. . . . However all this may be, it is certainly the case that art no longer affords that satisfaction of spiritual needs which earlier ages and nations sought in it, and found in it alone. . . . In all these respects art, considered in its highest vocation, is and remains for us a thing of the past. . . . For us art counts no longer as the highest mode in which truth fashions an existence for it-

self. . . . We may well hope that art will always rise higher and come to perfection, but the form of art has ceased to be the supreme need of the spirit.[2]

We try to neutralize this judgment by objecting, first of all, that at the very time when Hegel was writing its eulogy, art was producing countless masterpieces, and nearly as many aesthetic movements were starting; and, second, that his statement was dictated by the aim of preserving philosophy's preeminence among the other forms of absolute Spirit. However, those who have actually read the *Aesthetics* know that Hegel never denied the possibility of further development in art and that he thought of philosophy and art from a much too elevated perspective to let himself be guided by such "unphilosophical" motivations. On the contrary, we would have good reason not to take Hegel's word on the destiny of art too lightly: a thinker such as Heidegger, whose meditations on the problem of the relation between art and philosophy (which "remain close to each other though on the most separate peaks") represent perhaps the third and decisive event in the history of the διαφορά, took Hegel's lectures as his cue to ask whether "art [is] still an essential and necessary way in which that truth happens which is decisive for our historical existence."[3]

If we look more carefully at the text of the *Lectures on Aesthetics*, we find that Hegel does not speak anywhere of a "death" of art, or of an exhaustion or gradual extinguishing of its vital force; on the contrary, he says that "with the advance of civilization a time generally comes in the case of every people when art points beyond itself" and even speaks explicitly and more than once of an art that can "transcend itself."[4] Far from embodying an anti-artistic tendency with his judgment, as Croce feared, Hegel thinks about art in the most elevated manner possible, that is, *from the perspective of its self-transcendence*. His is in no way a simple eulogy, but is rather a meditation on the problem of art at the outer limit of its destiny, when art loosens itself from itself and moves in pure nothingness, suspended in a kind of diaphanous limbo between no-longer-being and not-yet-being.

What, then, does it mean that art has transcended itself? Does it really mean that art has become for us a thing of the past? That is has faded into the darkness of a final twilight? Or does it not rather mean that it has completed the circle of its metaphysical destiny and has reentered the dawn of an origin in which not only its destiny but the very destiny of man could be put in question in an initial manner?

In order to answer this question, we have to take a step back and return to what we wrote in the fourth chapter on the dissolution of the identity of artistic subjectivity with its subject matter. Going back, from the point of view of the artist, to the process that we have followed only from the point of view of the spectator, we have to ask what happens to the artist who, having become a *tabula rasa* in relation both to the matter and to the form of its production, discovers that no content is now immediately identified with his innermost consciousness.

It would appear at first blush that in contrast to the spectator, who confronts absolute otherness in the work of art, the artist possesses immediately his own principle in the act of creation and finds himself, to quote Rameau's nephew, as the only Memnon among so many puppets. But it is not so. What the artist experiences in the work of art is, in fact, that artistic subjectivity is absolute essence, for which all subject matter is indifferent; however, the pure creative-formal principle, split from any content, is the absolute abstract inessence, which annihilates and dissolves every content in its continuous effort to transcend and actualize itself. If the artist now seeks his certainty in a particular content or faith, he is lying, because he knows that pure artistic subjectivity is the essence of everything; but if he seeks his reality in pure artistic subjectivity, he finds himself in the paradoxical condition of having to find his own essence precisely in the inessential, his content in what is mere form. His condition, then, is that of a radical split; and, outside of this split, everything is a lie.

Faced with the transcendence of the creative-formal principle, the artist can of course surrender to its violence and try to live this principle as a new content in the general decline of all contents, trying to make of the split that inhabits him the fundamental experience starting from which a new human station becomes possible. He can, like Rimbaud, accept possession of himself only in extreme alienation, or, like Artaud, seek in the theatrical beyond of art the alchemical crucible in which man might finally refashion his body and reconcile his split. Yet, although he believes that he is now equal to his principle, and that in this attempt he has really penetrated a region where no other man would want to follow him, in proximity to a risk that threatens him more deeply than any other mortal being, still the artist remains on this side of his essence, since he has now definitively lost his content and is condemned forever to dwell, so to speak, beside his reality. The artist is the man without content, who has no other identity than a perpetual emerging out of the nothingness of expression and no other ground than this incomprehensible station on this side of himself.

The romantics, reflecting on this condition of the artist who has made in himself the experience of the infinite transcendence of the artistic principle, called *irony* the faculty through which he tears himself away from the world of contingencies and corresponds to that experience in the consciousness of his own absolute superiority on every content. *Irony* meant that art had to become its own object, and, no longer finding real seriousness in any content, could from now on only represent the negative potentiality of the poetic I, which, denying, continues to elevate itself beyond itself in an infinite doubling.

Baudelaire was aware of this paradoxical condition of the artist in the modern era, and in a short text bearing the apparently anodyne title "Of the Essence of Laughter," he left us a treatise on irony (called there the *comique absolu*) that takes Schlegel's theories to their extreme and deadly consequences. "Laughter," writes Baudelaire, "comes from the idea of our superiority," from the artist's transcendence with respect to himself. Properly speaking, he adds, laughter was unknown to the ancients, and it is reserved to our time, in which every artistic phenomenon is founded on the existence in the artist "of a permanent duality, the power to be at once oneself and another . . . the artist is artist only on condition of being double and of not ignoring any phenomenon of his double nature."[5]

Laughter is precisely the necessary result of this doubling. Caught in his infinite split, the artist is exposed to an extreme threat and ends up resembling Maturin's character Melmoth, who is condemned never to be able to free himself from the superiority he has acquired through a devilish pact: just like him, the artist "is a living contradiction. He has gone outside the fundamental conditions of life; his organs no longer bear his thought."[6]

Hegel was aware of this destructive vocation of irony. Analyzing Schlegel's theories in the *Aesthetics*, he saw in the omnilateral annihilation of all determinacy and all content an extreme reference of the subject to himself, that is, an extreme way of giving oneself self-consciousness. Yet he also understood that irony, on its destructive course, could not stop with the external world and was bound fatally to turn its negation against itself. The artistic subject, who has elevated himself like a god over his own creation, now accomplishes his negative work, destroying the very principle of negation: he is a god that destroys itself. To define this destiny of irony, Hegel uses the expression *ein Nichtiges, ein sich Vernichtendes*, "a self-annihilating nothing."[7] At the extreme limit of art's destiny, when all the gods fade in the twilight of art's laughter, art is only a negation that negates itself, a *self-annihilating nothing*.

If we now ask ourselves again, so what about art? what does it mean that art points beyond itself? we can perhaps answer: art does not die but, having become a self-annihilating nothing, eternally survives itself. Limitless, lacking content, double in its principle, it wanders in the nothingness of the *terra aesthetica*, in a desert of forms and contents that continually point it beyond its own image and which it evokes and immediately abolishes in the impossible attempt to found its own certainty. Its twilight can last more than the totality of its day, because its death is precisely its inability to die, its inability to measure itself to the essential origin of the work. Artistic subjectivity without content is now the pure force of negation that everywhere and at all times affirms only itself as absolute freedom that mirrors itself in pure self-consciousness. And, just as every content goes under in it, so the concrete space of the work disappears in it, the space in which once man's action and the world both found their reality in the image of the divine, and in which man's dwelling on earth used to take its diametrical measurement. In the pure self-supporting of the creative-formal principle, the sphere of the divine becomes opaque and withdraws, and it is in the experience of art that man becomes conscious, in the most radical way, of the event in which Hegel had already seen the most essential trait of unhappy consciousness, the event announced by Nietzsche's madman: "God is dead."[8]

Caught in the split of this consciousness, art does not die: on the contrary, it is precisely unable to die. Wherever art concretely seeks itself, the *Museum Theatrum* of aesthetics and criticism throws it back into the pure inessence of its principle. In the abstract pantheon of this empty self-consciousness, art gathers all the individual gods that have found in it their reality and their twilight, and its split penetrates now like a sole and immobile center the variety of figures and works that art has produced in the course of its becoming. The time of art has stopped, "but on the hour that contains in itself all the other hours on the dial, and consigns all of them to the lasting of an infinitely recurring instant."[9]

Inalienable and yet perpetually foreign to itself, art still wants and seeks its law, but because its link with the real world has grown weak, everywhere and on every occasion it wants the real precisely as Nothingness: art is the annihilating entity that traverses all its contents without ever being able to attain a positive work, because it cannot identify with any content. And since art has become the pure potentiality of negation, nihilism reigns in its essence. The kinship between art and nihilism, then, attains an inexpressibly deeper zone than that in which aestheticist and decadent poetics move. It unfolds its reign starting from the unthought foundation of Western art that has attained the extreme end of its metaphysical itinerary. And if the essence of nihilism does not consist simply in an inversion of accepted values, but remains veiled in the destiny of Western man and in the secret of his history, the destiny of art in our time is not something that can be decided on the ground of aesthetic criticism or linguistics. The essence of nihilism coincides with the essence of art at the extreme point of its destiny insofar as, in both, being destines itself to man in the form of Nothingness. And as long as nihilism secretly governs the course of Western history, art will not come out of its interminable twilight.

§ 7 Privation Is Like a Face

If the death of art is its inability to attain the concrete dimension of the work, the crisis of art in our time is, in reality, a crisis of poetry, of ποίησις. Ποίησις, poetry, does not designate here an art among others, but is the very name of man's *doing*, of that productive action of which artistic *doing* is only a privileged example, and which appears, today, to be unfolding its power on a planetary scale in the operation of technology and industrial production. The question about art's destiny here comes into contact with an area in which the entire sphere of human ποίησις, pro-ductive action in its entirety, is put into question in an original way. Today this pro-ductive doing, in the form of work, determines everywhere the status of man on earth, understood from the point of view of praxis, that is, of production of material life; and it is precisely because Marx's thought of the human condition and of human history is rooted in the alienated essence of this ποίησις and experiences the "degrading division of labor into intellectual and manual labor" that it is still relevant today. What, then, does ποίησις, poetry, mean? What does it mean that man has on earth a poetic, that is, a pro-ductive, status?

In the *Symposium* Plato tells us about the full original resonance of the word ποίησις: "any cause that brings into existence something that was not there before is Ποίησις."[1] Every time that something is pro-duced, that is, brought from concealment and nonbeing into the light of presence, there is ποίησις, pro-duction, po-etry.² In this broad original sense of the word, every art—not only the verbal kind—is poetry, pro-duction into presence, and the ac-tivity of the craftsman who makes an object is ποίησις as well. To the extent that in it everything brings itself spontaneously into presence, even nature, φύσις, has the character of ποίησις.

In the second book of the *Physics*, however, Aristotle distin-guishes between that which, existing by nature (φύσει), contains in itself its own ἀρχή, that is, the principle and origin of its entry into presence, and that which, existing from other causes (δι᾿ἄλλας αἰτίας), does not have its principle in itself but finds it in the pro-ductive activity of man.³ Of this second category of things, the Greeks said that it is—that it enters into presence—ἀπὸ τέχνης, from or starting out from *technics*, from skill, and τέχνη was the name that designated both the activity of the craftsman who shapes a vase and that of the artist who molds a statue or writes a poem. Both of these forms of activity had in common the essential char-acter of being a species of ποίησις, of the pro-duction into pres-ence. This *poietic* character related them back to φύσις, nature, while yet distinguishing them from it, since nature is intended as that which contains in itself the principle of its own entry into presence. On the other hand, according to Aristotle, the pro-duc-tion worked by ποίησις always has the character of the installation into a shape (μορφὴ καὶ εἶδος)—in the sense that the transition from nonbeing to being means taking on a form, a shape—because it is precisely in a shape and starting from a shape that whatever is pro-duced enters into presence.

If we now turn from Greece to our times, we notice that this unitary status of the things not coming from nature (μὴ φύσει ὄντα) as τέχνη is broken. With the development of modern tech-nology, starting with the first industrial revolution in the second half of the eighteenth century, and with the establishment of an ever more widespread and alienating division of labor, the mode of presence of the things pro-duced by man becomes double: on the one hand there are the things that enter into presence according to the statute of aesthetics, that is, the works of art, and on the other hand there are those that come into being by way of τέχνη, that is, products in the strict sense. Ever since the beginning of aesthetics, the particular status of the works of art among the things that do not contain their own ἀρχή in themselves has been identified with originality (or authenticity).

What does *originality* mean? When we say that the work of art has the character of originality (or authenticity), we do not simply mean by this that this work is unique, that is, different from any other. Originality means proximity to the origin. The work of art is original because it maintains a particular relationship to its origin, to its formal ἀρχή, in the sense that it not only derives from the latter and conforms to it but also remains in a relationship of permanent proximity to it.

In other words, originality means that the work of art—which, to the extent that it has the character of ποίησις, is pro-duced into presence in a shape and from a shape—maintains with its formal principle such a relation of proximity as excludes the possibility that its entry into presence may be in some way reproducible, almost as though the shape pro-duced itself into presence in the unrepeatable act of aesthetic creation.

Things that come into being according to τέχνη, on the other hand, do not have this relationship of proximity with the εἶδος, the image, which governs and determines the entry into presence; the εἶδος, the formal principle, is simply the external paradigm, the mold (τύπος) to which the product must conform in order to come into being, while the poietic act can be reproduced indefinitely (at least as long as the material possibility of doing so remains). *Reproducibility (intended, in this sense, as paradigmatic relationship of non-proximity with the origin) is, then, the essential status of the product of technics, while originality (or authenticity) is the essential status of the work of art.* If the dual status of man's pro-ductive activity is conceived as starting from the division of labor, it can be explained in this way: the privileged status of art in the aesthetic sphere is artificially interpreted as the survival of a condition in which manual and intellectual labor are not yet divided and in which, therefore, the productive act maintains all its integrity and uniqueness; by contrast, technical production, which takes place starting from a condition of extreme division of labor, remains essentially fungible and reproducible.

The existence of a dual status for man's poietic activity appears so natural to us now that we forget that the entrance of the work of art into the aesthetic dimension is a relatively recent event, and one that, when it took place, introduced a radical split in the spiritual life of the artist, changing substantially the aspect of humanity's cultural pro-duction. Among the first consequences of this split was the rapid eclipse of those sciences, such as rhetoric and dogmatics, of those social institutions, such as workshops and art schools, and of those structures of artistic composition, such as the repetition of styles, iconographic continuity, and the required tropes of literary composition, that were based precisely on the existence of a unitary status for human ποίησις. The doctrine of originality literally exploded the condition of the artist. Everything that in some way constituted the common space in which the personalities of different artists met in a living unity in order then to assume, within the strictures of this common mold, their unmistakable physiognomy became a *commonplace* in the pejorative sense, an unbearable encumbrance: the artist in whom the modern critical demon has insinuated itself must free himself from it or perish.

In the revolutionary enthusiasm that accompanied this process, few recognized the negative consequences that it threatened to have for the condition of the artist himself, who inevitably lost even the possibility of a concrete social status. In his "Remarks on 'Oedipus,'" Hölderlin foresaw this danger and sensed that art would soon find itself in need of reacquiring the craftsmanship it had had in more ancient times:

> It will be good, in order to secure for today's poets a bourgeois existence—taking into account the difference of times and institutions—if we elevate poetry today to the *mechane* of the ancients. When being compared with those of the Greeks, other works of art, too, lack reliability; at least, they have been judged until today according to the impressions which they made rather than according to their lawful calculation and their other modes of operation through which the beau-

tiful is engendered. Modern poetry, however, lacks especially training and craftsmanship, namely, that its mode of operation can be calculated and taught and, once it has been learned, is always capable of being repeated reliably in practice.[4]

If we now look at contemporary art, we notice that the need for a unitary status has become so strong that, at least in its most significant forms, it appears to be based precisely on an intentional confusion and perversion of the two spheres of ποίησις. The need for authenticity in technical production and that for reproducibility of artistic creation have given birth to two hybrid forms, the "ready-made" and pop art, which lay bare the split inherent in man's poietic activity.

As is well known, Duchamp took a common product, such as anyone could purchase in a department store, and, alienating it from its natural environment, forced it into the sphere of art in a sort of gratuitous act. That is, with a creative play on the existence of a double status in man's creative activity, he transferred the object from a technically reproducible and fungible state to one of aesthetic authenticity and uniqueness—at least for the brief instant during which the estrangement effect lasts.

Like the "ready-made," pop art is based on a perversion of the double status of aesthetic activity, but in it the phenomenon appears reversed, and rather resembles that "reciprocal ready-made" that Duchamp had in mind when he suggested that one use a Rembrandt as an ironing board. *While the "ready-made" proceeds from the sphere of the technical product to the sphere of art, pop art moves in the opposite direction: from aesthetic status to the status of industrial product.* While in the "ready-made" the spectator was faced with an object existing according to technics that was inexplicably charged with a certain potential of aesthetic authenticity, in pop art the spectator is confronted with a work of art that appears denuded of its aesthetic potential and that paradoxically assumes the status of the industrial product.

In both cases—except for the instant of the alienation effect—the passage from the one to the other status is impossible: that which is reproducible cannot become original, and that which is irreproducible cannot be reproduced. The object cannot attain presence and remains enveloped in shadow, suspended in a kind of disquieting limbo between being and nonbeing. It is precisely this inability of the object to attain presence that endows both the "ready-made" and pop art with their enigmatic meaning.

In other words, both forms push the split we have been talking about to its extreme point, and in this way point beyond aesthetics to an area (still in shadow) in which the pro-ductive activity of man may become reconciled with itself. However, it is the very poietic substance of man that is brought to a crisis point in both cases: that ποίησις of which Plato said that "any cause that brings into existence something that was not there before is ποίησις." In the "ready-made" and in pop art, nothing comes into presence if not the privation of a potentiality that cannot find its reality anywhere. "Ready-made" and pop art, then, constitute the most alienated (and thus the most extreme) form of ποίησις, the form in which privation itself comes into presence. In the crepuscular light of this presence-absence, the question on the fate of art now sounds as follows: how is it possible to attain a new ποίησις in an original way?

If we now attempt to come closer to the meaning of this extreme destiny of ποίησις by which it dispenses its power only as privation (though this privation is also, in reality, an extreme gift of poetry, the most accomplished and charged with meaning, because in it nothingness itself is called into presence), we must interrogate the work, because it is in the work that ποίησις actualizes its power. What, then, is the character of the work, in which the pro-ductive activity of man concretizes itself?

For Aristotle, the pro-duction into presence, effected by ποίησις both for the things whose ἀρχή is in man and for those that exist according to nature, has the character of ἐνέργεια. This word is usually translated as "actual reality," contrasting with "potentiality," but in this translation the original sonority of the word remains veiled. To indicate the same concept, Aristotle also employs a term he himself coined: ἐντελέχεια. That which enters into presence and remains in presence, gathering itself, in an end-directed way, into a shape in which it finds its fullness, its completeness; that which, then, ἐν τέλει ἔχει, possesses itself in its own end, has the character of ἐνέργεια. Ἐνέργεια, then, means being-at-work, ἐν ἔργον, since the work, ἔργον, is precisely *entelechy*, that which enters into presence and lasts by gathering itself into its own shape as into its own end.

Opposed to ἐνέργεια in Aristotle is δύναμις (Latin: *potentia*), which characterizes the mode of presence of that which, not being at work, does not yet possess itself in its own shape as in its own end, but exists simply in the mode of availability, of being useful for . . . , as a plank in a carpenter's workshop or a marble block in a sculptor's studio is available for the poietic act that will make it appear as a table or a statue.

The work, the result of ποίησις, can never be only potential, because it is precisely pro-duction into and station in a shape that possesses itself in its own end. It is for this reason that Aristotle writes, "we would never say that something exists according to τέχνη if, for example, something is a bed only in availability and potentiality (δύναμει), but does not have the shape of the bed."[5]

If we now consider the double status of the poietic activity of modern man, we will see that, while the work of art has *par excellence* the character of ἐνέργεια, that is, possesses itself in the unrepeatability of its formal εἶδος as in its end, the product of technology lacks this energetic station in its own form, as though the character of availability ended up by obscuring its formal aspect. Of course the industrial product is finished, in the sense that the productive process has come to its end, but the particular relationship of distance from its principle of origin—in other words, its reproducibility—causes the product never to possess itself in its own shape as in its own end, and thus the product remains in a condition of perpetual potentiality. That is, *the entry into presence has the character of ἐνέργεια, of being-at-work, in the work of art, and the character of δύναμις, of availability for . . . in the industrial product* (we usually express this by saying that the industrial product is not a "work" but, precisely, a product).

But is the energetic status of the work of art in the aesthetic dimension in fact such? Ever since our relationship with the work of art was reduced (or, if you wish, purified) to mere aesthetic enjoyment achieved through good taste, the status of the work itself has been imperceptibly changing under our very eyes. We see that museums and galleries stock and accumulate works of art so that they may be available at any moment for the spectator's aesthetic enjoyment, more or less as happens with raw materials or with merchandise accumulated in a warehouse. Wherever a work of art is pro-duced and exhibited today, its *energetic* aspect, that is, the being-at-work of the work, is erased to make room for its character as a stimulant of the aesthetic sentiment, as mere support of aesthetic enjoyment. In the work of art, in other words, the dynamic character of its availability for aesthetic enjoyment obscures the *energetic* character of its final station in its own shape. If this is true, then even the work of art, in the dimension of aesthetics, has, like the product of technics, the character of δύναμις, of availability for . . . , and *the split in the unitary status of man's pro-ductive ability marks in reality his passage from the sphere of ἐνέργεια to that of δύναμις, from being-at-work to mere potentiality.*

The rise of the poetics of the open work and of the work-in-progress, founded not on an energetic but on a dynamic status of the work of art, signifies precisely this extreme moment of the exile of the work of art from its essence, the moment in which—having become pure potentiality, mere being-available in itself and for itself—it consciously takes on its own inability to possess itself in its end. "Open work" means: work that does not possess itself in its own εἶδος as in its end, work that is never at work, that is (if it is true that work is ἐνέργεια), nonwork, δύναμις, availability, and potentiality.

Precisely because it is in the mode of availability for . . . , because it plays more or less consciously on the aesthetic status of the work of art as mere availability for aesthetic enjoyment, the open work constitutes not a surpassing of aesthetics but only one of the forms of its fulfillment, and points beyond aesthetics only negatively.

In the same way, the "ready-made" and pop art play on the double status of the productive activity of the man of our time, perverting it; thus, they are also in the mode of δύναμις, and of a δύναμις that can never possess itself in its end. Yet precisely because they escape both the aesthetic enjoyment of the work of art and the consumption of the technical product, they actualize at least for an instant a suspension of these two statuses, push the consciousness of laceration much further than does the open work, and present themselves as a true availability-toward-nothingness. Since they properly belong neither to artistic activity nor to technical production, nothing in them really comes into being; likewise, one can say that since they offer themselves neither for aesthetic enjoyment nor for consumption, in their case availability and potentiality are turned toward nothingness, and in this way they are able to possess-themselves-in-their-end.

Availability-toward-nothingness, although it is not yet work, is in some way a negative presence, a shadow of being-at-work: it is ~~ἐνέργεια~~, ~~work~~, and as such constitutes the most urgent critical appeal that the artistic consciousness of our time has expressed toward the alienated essence of the work of art. The split in the productive activity of man, the "degrading division of labor into manual and intellectual work," is not overcome here but rather made extreme. Yet it is also starting from this self-suppression of the privileged status of "artistic work," which now gathers the two sides of the halved apple of human pro-duction in their irreconcilable opposition, that it will be possible to exit the swamp of aesthetics and technics and restore to the poetic status of man on earth its original dimension.

§ 8 Poiesis and Praxis

It may be time to attempt a more original understanding of the statement made in the previous chapter: "man has on earth a poetic, that is, a pro-ductive, status." The problem of the destiny of art in our time has led us to posit as inseparable from it the problem of the meaning of productive activity, of man's "doing" in its totality. This productive activity is understood, in our time, as praxis. According to current opinion, all of man's doing—that of the artist and the craftsman as well as that of the workman and the politician—is praxis, that is, manifestation of a will that produces a concrete effect. When we say that man has a productive status on earth, we mean, then, that the status of his dwelling on earth is a *practical* one.

We are so accustomed to this unified understanding of all of man's "doing" as praxis that we do not recognize that it could be, and in other eras has been, conceived differently. The Greeks, to whom we owe all the categories through which we judge ourselves and the reality around us, made a clear distinction between *poiesis* (*poiein*, "to pro-duce" in the sense of bringing into being) and *praxis* (*prattein*, "to do" in the sense of acting). As we shall see, central to praxis was the idea of the will that finds its immediate expression in an act, while, by contrast, central to poiesis was the experience of pro-duction into presence, the fact that something passed from nonbeing to being, from concealment into the full light of the work. The essential character of poiesis was not its aspect as a practical and voluntary process but its being a mode of truth understood as unveiling, ἀ-λήθεια. And it was precisely because of this essential proximity to truth that Aristotle, who repeatedly theorizes this distinction within man's "doing," tended to assign a higher position to poiesis than to praxis. According to Aristotle, the roots of praxis lay in the very condition of man as an *animal*, a living being: these roots were constituted by the very principle of motion (will, understood as the basic unit of craving, desire, and volition) that characterizes life.

The Greeks were prevented from considering work thematically, as one of the fundamental modes of human activity besides poiesis and praxis, by the fact that the physical work necessary for life's needs was performed by slaves. However, this does not mean that they were unaware of its existence or had not understood its nature. To work meant to submit to necessity, and submission to necessity, which made man the equal of the animal, with its perpetual and forced search for means of sustenance, was thought incompatible with the condition of the free man. As Hannah Arendt rightly points out, to affirm that work was an object of contempt in antiquity because it was reserved to slaves is a prejudice: the ancients reasoned about it in the opposite direction, deeming necessary the existence of slaves because of the slavish nature of the activities that provided for life's sustenance. In other words, they had understood one of the essential characteristics of work, namely, its immediate relation to the biological process of life. For while poiesis constructs the space where man finds his certitude and where he ensures the freedom and duration of his action, the presupposition of work is, on the contrary, bare biological existence, the cyclical processes of the human body, whose metabolism and whose energy depend on the basic products of labor.[1]

In the Western cultural tradition, the distinction between these three kinds of human doing—poiesis, praxis, and work—has been progressively obscured. What the Greeks conceived as poiesis is understood by the Romans as one mode of *agere*, that is, as an acting that puts-to-work, an *operari*. Ἔργον and ἐνέργεια, which for the

Greeks had nothing directly to do with action but rather designated the essential character of a status in presence, become in Latin *actus* and *actualitas*: they are transposed (trans-lated) into the plane of *agere*, of the voluntary production of an effect. Christian theological thought, which conceived the supreme Being as an *actus purus*, ties to Western metaphysics the interpretation of being as actuality and act. When this process is completed in the modern era, every chance to distinguish between poiesis and praxis, pro-duction and action, is lost. Man's "doing" is determined as an activity producing a real effect (the *opus* of *operari*, the *factum* of *facere*, the *actus* of *agere*), whose worth is appreciated with respect to the will that is expressed in it, that is, with respect to its freedom and creativity. The central experience of poiesis, pro-duction into presence, is replaced by the question of the "how," that is, of the process through which the object has been produced. In terms of the work of art, this means that the emphasis shifts away from what the Greeks considered the essence of the work—the fact that in it something passed from nonbeing into being, thus opening the space of truth (ἀ-λήθεια) and building a world for man's dwelling on earth—and to the *operari* of the artist, that is, to the creative genius and the particular characteristics of the artistic process in which it finds expression.

In a movement parallel to this process of convergence between poiesis and praxis, work, which used to occupy the lowest rank in the hierarchy of active life, climbs to the rank of central value and common denominator of every human activity. This ascent begins at the moment when Locke discovers in work the origin of property, continues when Adam Smith elevates it to the source of all wealth, and reaches its peak with Marx, who makes of it the expression of man's very humanity.[2] At this point, all human "doing" is interpreted as praxis, as concrete productive activity (in opposition to theory, understood as a synonym of thought and abstract meditation), and praxis is conceived in turn as starting from work, that is, from the production of material life that corresponds to life's biological cycle. This productive doing now everywhere determines the status of man on earth—man understood as the living being (*animal*) that works (*laborans*), and, in work, produces himself and ensures his dominion over the earth. Everywhere, even where Marx's thought is condemned and refused, man today is the living being who produces and works. And artistic pro-duction, which has now become creative activity, also enters into the dimension of praxis, albeit a very peculiar praxis, aesthetic creation or superstructure.

In the course of this process, which implies a total reversal of the traditional hierarchy of man's activities, one thing remains unchanged, namely, the taking root of praxis in biological existence, which Aristotle had expressed by interpreting its principle as will, drive, and vital impulse. The ascent of work from the lowest to the highest rank and the subsequent eclipse of the sphere of poiesis depended precisely on the fact that the endless process put into being by work was, among all human activities, the most directly tied to the biological cycle of the organism.

All the attempts made in the modern era to found man's "doing" differently have remained anchored to this interpretation of praxis as will and vital impulse—that is, to an interpretation of life, of man as a living being. In our time, the philosophy of man's "doing" continues to be a philosophy of life. Even when Marx inverts the traditional hierarchy of theory and praxis, the Aristotelian determination of praxis as will remains unchanged, because for Marx work is, in its essence, "capacity for work" (*Arbeitskraft*), and its foundation is inherent in the very natural character of man as "active natural being," that is, as endowed with vital instincts and appetites.

In the same way, all attempts to transcend aesthetics and to give a new status to artistic pro-duction have started from the blurring of the distinction between poiesis and praxis, that is, from the interpretation of art as a mode of praxis and of praxis as the expression of a will and a creative force. Novalis's definition of poetry as a "willful, active, and productive use of our organs,"[3] Nietzsche's identification of art with the will to power in the idea of the universe "as a work of art that gives birth to itself," Artaud's aspiration to a theatrical liberation of the will, and the situationist project of an overcoming of art based on a practical actualization of the cre-

ative impulses that are expressed in art in an alienated fashion, are
all tributary to a determination of the essence of human activity as
will and vital impulse, and are therefore founded in the forgetting
of the original pro-ductive status of the work of art as foundation
of the space of truth. The point of arrival of Western aesthetics is a
metaphysics of the will, that is, of life understood as energy and
creative impulse.

This metaphysics of the will has penetrated our conception of
art to such an extent that even the most radical critiques of aesthetics have not questioned its founding principle, that is, the idea
that art is the expression of the artist's creative will. Such critiques
remain inside aesthetics, since they are only the extreme development of one of the two polarities on which it founds its interpretation of the work of art: the polarity of genius understood as will
and creative force. And yet what the Greeks meant with the distinction between poiesis and praxis was precisely that the essence
of poiesis has nothing to do with the expression of a will (with respect to which art is in no way necessary): this essence is found instead in the production of truth and in the subsequent opening of
a world for man's existence and action.

In what follows, I will ask about the relation between poiesis and
praxis in Western thought and attempt to sketch its evolution,
pointing to the process through which the work of art crosses over
from the sphere of poiesis to that of praxis and eventually finds its
status in a metaphysics of the will, that is, of life and its creativity.

1. "The Genus of Poiesis Is Different from That of Praxis"

As we saw in the previous chapter, the Greeks used the word
ποίησις to characterize τέχνη, human pro-duction in its entirety,
and designated with the same name of τεχνίτης both the craftsman and the artist. But this common designation does not in any
way suggest that the Greeks conceived of pro-duction from its material and practical side, as a manual making; what they called
τέχνη was neither the actualization of a will nor simply a con-

structing, but a mode of truth, of ἀ-ληθεύειν, of the unveiling that produces things from concealment into presence.

In other words, τέχνη meant for the Greeks "to cause to appear," and ποίησις meant "pro-duction into presence"; but this production was not understood in connection with *agere*, doing, but with γνῶσις, knowing.[4] Conceived in a Greek fashion, pro-duction (ποίησις, τέχνη) and praxis are not the same thing.

In the *Nicomachean Ethics*, in the course of a famous classification of the "dispositions" through which the soul attains truth, Aristotle distinguishes sharply between ποίησις and πρᾶξις ("the genus of action is different from that of pro-duction, for while production has an end other than itself, action cannot; for good action is itself its end").[5]

The essence of pro-duction, conceived in the Greek way, is to bring something into presence (this is why Aristotle says ἔστι δε τέχνη πᾶσα περὶ γένεσιν, "every art is concerned with giving birth"). Consequently, it necessarily has both its end and its limit outside itself (τέλος and πέρας, "limit," are the same thing in Greek; cf. Aristotle, *Metaphysics* IV, 1022b): end and limit are not identified with the act of production itself. In other words, the way the Greeks thought of production and the work of art was the inverse of the way in which aesthetics has accustomed us to think of them: ποίησις is not an end in itself and does not contain its own limit, because it does not bring itself into presence in the work, as acting (πρᾶξις) brings itself into presence in the act (πρακτόν); the work of art is not the result of a doing, not the *actus* of an *agere*, but something substantially other (ἕτερον) than the principle that has pro-duced it into presence. Art's entry into the aesthetic dimension is thus possible only because art itself has already left the sphere of pro-duction, of ποίησις, to enter that of praxis.

But if ποιεῖν and πράττειν are not the same thing for the Greeks, what then is the essence of πρᾶξις? The word πρᾶξις comes from πείρω, to cross, and is etymologically linked to πέρα (beyond), πόρος (passage, door) and πέρας (limit). It suggests *passing through*, a passage that goes up to the πέρας, to the limit. Πέρας here has the meaning of end, close, extreme point, τὸ τέλος ἑκάστου (Aristotle, *Metaphysics* V, 1022a), that is, that toward which motion and action proceed; and this end, as we have seen, is not external to action but inherent in it. An English word that, considered etymologically, corresponds to πράξις, is *experience, ex-per-ientia*, which contains the same idea of a *going through* of action and in the action. The Greek word that corresponds to the word "experience"— ἐμπειρία—contains the same root as πράξις, namely περ, πείρω, πέρας: etymologically speaking it is the same word.

Aristotle hints at an affinity between experience and praxis when he says, "with a view to action [το πράττειν], experience [ἐμπειρία] seems in no respect inferior to art [τέχνη] . . . since experience is knowledge of individuals, while art is knowledge of universals, and action [πράξις] . . . is concerned with the individual."[6] In the same passage, Aristotle also says that animals have impressions and memory (φαντασίαι καὶ μνήμη) but not experience, while man is capable of ἐμπειρία and, thanks to it, has art and science (ἐπιστήμη καὶ τέχνη). Experience, Aristotle adds, looks very similar to art, but differs from it in substantial ways: "For to have a judgement that when Callias was ill of this disease this did him good, and similarly in the case of Socrates and in many individual cases, is a matter of experience; but to judge that it has done good to all persons of a certain constitution, marked off in one class, when they were ill of this disease . . . , this is a matter of art [τέχνη]."[7] Aristotle characterizes practical knowledge in a similar way, explaining that while the object of theory is truth, the object of practice is action, "for even if they consider how things are, practical men do not study the eternal, but what is relative [πρός τι] and in the present [νῦν]."[8] If all intellectual activity is either practical or pro-ductive or theoretical (πᾶσα διάνοια ἢ πρακτικὴ ἢ ποιητικὴ ἢ θεωρετική—*Metaphysics* VI 1025b), experience is then διάνοια πρακτική, νοῦς πρακτικός, practical intellect, ability to determine this or that individual action. That only man is capable of experience means, then, that only man determines, that is, traverses his action, and is therefore capable of πράξις, of the *going through all the way to the action's limit* (where the genitive "action's" has both objective and subjective value).

Ἐμπειρία and πρᾶξις, then, belong to the same process, and ἐμπειρία is νοῦς πρακτικός; yet, if it is so, what is their relationship within this process, and, better, what is the principle that determines both? The answer that Aristotle offers for this problem at the end of his treatise *On the Soul* has had a decisive influence on all that Western philosophy has conceived as praxis and human activity.

The treatise *On the Soul* characterizes the living being as that which moves by itself, and man's movement as a living being is πρᾶξις. Seeking a solution to the problem of what might be the moving principle of praxis, Aristotle writes:

> Both of these then are capable of originating local movement, thought and will [ἡ ὄρεξις] . . . ; that which is the object of will is the originating principle of practical thought [ἀρχὴ τοῦ πρακτικοῦ νοῦ]; and the latter is the originating principle of praxis [ἀρχὴ τῆς πράξεως]. It follows that there is a justification for regarding these two as the sources of movement, i.e. will and practical thought; for the object of will starts a movement and practical thought moves because its principle [ἀρχή] is the object of will. . . . As it is, the mind is never found producing movement without the will (for deliberating volition [βούλησις] is a form of will; and when movement is produced according to calculation it is also produced according to will). . . . It is clear then . . . that will originates movement.⁹

The determining principle (ἀρχή) of praxis as well as of practical thought is, then, the will (ὄρεξις), intended in its broadest sense and therefore including ἐπιθυμία, longing, θύμος, desire, and βούλησις, volition; that man is capable of praxis means that man wills his action and, willing it, goes through it to its limit. Praxis is *going through to the limit of the action, while moved by will*; it is willed action.

However, the will does not simply move, it is not an immobile motor; rather it moves and is moved (κινεῖ καὶ κινεῖται), it is itself movement (κίνησίς τις). That is, will is not simply the moving principle of praxis, not only that out of which praxis moves or originates; rather, will traverses and sustains action from the beginning to the end of its entry into presence. *Through action, it is the will that moves and reaches its own limit.* Praxis is will that traverses and traces its circle all the way to its limit: πράξις is ὄρεξις, will and longing.

Praxis, thus understood as will, remains for the Greeks sharply distinct from ποίησις, pro-duction. Pro-duction has its πέρας, its limit, outside itself; that is, it is pro-ductive, it is the original principle (ἀρχή) of something other than itself. By contrast, the will that is at the origin of praxis and reaches its limit in action, remains enclosed in its circle. It wants only itself through action; thus it is not pro-ductive, and brings only itself into presence.

2. "Poetic Art Is Nothing but a Willful, Active, and Productive Use of Our Organs"

The Aristotelian interpretation of praxis as will traverses the history of Western thought from end to end. In the course of this history, as we have seen, ἐνέργεια becomes *actualitas*, actuality and reality, and its essence is coherently regarded as an *agere*, an *actus*. The essence of this *agere* is interpreted in turn according to the Aristotelian model of the reciprocal belonging of ὄρεξις and νοῦς πρακτικός, as will and representation. It is in this way that Leibniz conceives the being of the monad as *vis primitiva activa* (primitive active force) and determines *agere* as the union of *perceptio* and *appetitus*, perception and will, and that Kant and Fichte think reason as freedom, and freedom as will.

Taking up Leibniz's distinction between *appetitus* and *perceptio*, Schelling gives this metaphysics of will a formulation that will exert great influence on the Jena romantics. In *Of Human Freedom* he writes: "In the final and highest instance there is no other Being than will. Will is primordial Being [*Ur-sein*], and all predicates apply to it alone—groundlessness [*Grundlosigkeit*], eternity, independence of time, self-affirmation [*Selbstbejahung*]. All philosophy strives only to find its highest expression."[10]

But Schelling does more than just absolutize will by making it into the original principle. He determines the being of will as pure will, will that wants itself, and this "will of will" is the *Ur-grund*, the original ground, or, better, the *Un-grund*, the without-ground, the shapeless and dark abyss, the "hunger to be" that exists before any opposition and without which nothing can come into existence. "In origin," he writes, "the spirit, in the broadest sense of the world, is not theoretical in nature . . . originally it is rather *will*, and a will merely for will, a will that wants not something, but only itself." Man, who partakes both of this original abyss and of spiritual existence, is the "central being" (*Zentralwesen*), the mediator between God and Nature; he is "the redeemer of nature towards whom all its archetypes strive."[11]

This idea of man as the redeemer and messiah of nature is developed by Novalis in the form of an interpretation of science, art, and in general all of human activity as the "formation" or "education" (*Bildung*) of nature, in a sense that appears to anticipate Marx's thought and in some ways Nietzsche's as well. Novalis's project is to go beyond Fichte's idealism, which revealed to man the power of the thinking spirit.

As Marx would do fifty years later, however, Novalis located this "going beyond" in praxis, understood as a higher unity of thought and action that gives man the means to transform the world and reintegrate the Golden Age. "Fichte," he writes, "has taught and discovered the active use of the mental organ. But has he discovered the laws of the active use of organs in general?" (frag. 1681). Just as we move our mental organ as we please and translate its movements into language and willful acts, so we should learn to move the internal organs of our body and the body itself as a whole. Only in this way would man become truly independent from nature and only so would he be able to force the senses to "*produce* for him the shape that he desires, and he could, in the strict sense of the term, live in *his* world." The fate that has burdened man up to now is merely the laziness of his spirit;

> yet, broadening and shaping our activity, we will ourselves become destiny. It appears that everything flows toward us from the outside, because we do not flow toward the outside. We are negative because we want to be—the more positive we become, the more the world

around us will become negative—until at the end there will be no more negation and we will be everything in everything. *God wants gods.* (frag. 1682)

This "art of becoming all-powerful" through an active use of the organs consists in the appropriation of our body and of its creative organic activity: "The body is the instrument of the formation and modification of the world. Thus we must make of our body an organ *capable of everything*. Modifying our instrument means modifying the world" (frag. 1684).

If this appropriation were to take place, the reconciliation of spirit and nature, of will and accident, of theory and practice, in a superior unity, an "absolute, practical and empirical I" (frag. 1668) would also occur. Novalis calls this higher praxis Poetry (*Poesie*) and defines it as follows: "Poetic art is only—a willful, active, and productive use of our organs" (frag. 1339). A fragment from 1789 reveals the proper meaning of this higher praxis: "Everything that is *involuntary* [*unwillkürlich*] must become *willful* [*willkürlich*]" (frag. 1686).

The principle of Poetry, in which the unity of theory and practice, of spirit and nature, is actualized, is will, and not the will of something but absolute will, the will of will, in the sense in which Schelling had determined the original abyss: "I know myself as I want myself, and want myself as I know myself—because I *want* my *will*, because I want absolutely. Consequently, in me knowing and willing are perfectly unified" (frag. 1670). The man who has raised himself to this higher praxis is nature's messiah, whose world is conjoined with the divine world and finds its most proper meaning: "Humanity is so to speak the higher meaning of our planet, the eye that it raises to the sky, the nerve that links this limb to the higher world" (frag. 1680).

At the end of this process, man and the becoming of the world become identical to each other in the circle of absolute and unconditional will, a circle in whose Golden Age it already seems possible to hear Zarathustra's message, the message of the one who, in the great midday of humanity, teaches the eternal recurrence of the identical: "Everything that happens, *I want*. Willful phlegm. Active use of the senses" (frag. 1730).

3. "Man Produces Universally"

Marx thinks of man's being as production. Production means praxis, "sensuous human activity." What is the character of this activity? While the animal, writes Marx, is immediately at one with its vital activity, *is* its vital activity, man does not confuse himself with it; he turns his vital activity into a means for his existence. He produces not unilaterally but universally. "It is for this very and only reason that he is a being belonging to a genus [*Gattungswesen*]."[12] Praxis constitutes man in his proper being: it makes a *Gattungswesen* of him. The character of production, then, is to constitute man as a being capable of a genus; it is to give him the gift of a genus (*Gattung*). Yet Marx adds immediately afterward: "Rather, [man] is a conscious being, that is, his life is an object for him, precisely because he is a *Gattungswesen*, a being belonging to a genus." Man, then, is not a *Gattungswesen* to the extent that he is a producer; on the contrary, it is his quality as a generic being that makes a producer of him. Marx reasserts this essential ambiguity when he writes that, on the one hand, "the practical creation *of an objective world*, the *transformation* of inorganic nature, is proof that man is a *Gattungswesen*" (*MEGA*, p. 369) but that, on the other hand, "precisely in the transformation of the objective world man proves himself for the first time a *Gattungswesen*" (*MEGA*, p. 370).

We face here a real hermeneutic circle: on the one hand, production, man's conscious vital activity, constitutes him into a being capable of a genus, but on the other hand it is his capacity to have a genus that makes a producer of him. That this circle is neither a contradiction nor a result of a lack of rigor, that instead an essential moment of Marx's reflection is contained there, is proven by the way in which Marx himself appears aware of the reciprocal belonging of praxis and "genus life" (*Gattungsleben*): he writes that "the object of labor is the *objectification of genus life*," and that "alienated labor, since it takes away from man the object of his production, takes away from him also his genus life, his actual generic objectivity [*Gattungsgegenständlichkeit*]" (*MEGA*, p. 370).

Thus praxis and genus life belong reciprocally to each other in a circle within which each is the origin and foundation of the other. It is only because Marx thoroughly experienced this circle in his thought that he was able to distance himself from Feuerbach's "intuitive materialism" (*anschauende Materialismus*) and to think of "sensibility" as practical activity, as praxis. That is, thinking through this circle is precisely the original experience of Marx's thought. What, then, does *Gattung*, genus, mean? What does it mean that man is a *Gattungswesen*, a being capable of genus?

The usual translation of this expression is "a generic being" or "a being belonging to a species" in the sense, derived from the natural sciences, that the words "species" and "genus" have in everyday speech. But *Gattung* does not mean only "natural species": this is proven by Marx's assertion that the quality of *Gattungswesen* is precisely the characteristic that distinguishes men from other animals, and by his explicit linking of it to praxis, to the conscious vital activity proper to man, and not to the vital activity of animals. If only man is a *Gattungswesen*, if only man is capable of genus, the word "genus" here clearly has a deeper meaning than the usual naturalistic one, and this meaning cannot be understood in its own resonance if it is not put in relation with the role of this word in the thought of Western philosophy.

In the fifth book of the *Metaphysics*, which is entirely devoted to the explanation of several terms, Aristotle defines genus (γένος) as γένεσις συνεχής. Thus—he adds—the expression "so long as the human genus exists" means "so long as there is γένεσις συνεχής of men" (*Metaphysics* 1024a). The usual translation of γένεσις συνεχής is "continuous generation," but this translation is correct only if we understand "generation" in its broader sense as "origin," and if we also read in the word "continuous" not only "compact, uninterrupted" but, according to its etymology, "that which holds together (συν-έχει), con-tinens, that which con-tains and contains itself." Γένεσις συνεχής means: the origin that holds together (συν-έχει) in presence. Genus (γένος) is the *original con-tainer* (both in the active sense of that which holds together and gathers, and in the reflexive sense of that which holds itself together and is continuous) of the individuals who belong to it.

That man is capable of genus, that he is a *Gattungswesen*, means then: there is for man an *original container*, a principle that causes men not to be foreign to one another but to be, indeed, *human*, in the sense that in every man the whole genus is immediately and necessarily present. This is why Marx can say that "man is a *Gattungswesen* . . . because he behaves toward himself as he does toward the present and living genus" and that "the statement that man is made foreign to his generic being means that each man has become foreign to every other man, and at the same time that each man has become foreign to man's being" (*MEGA*, p. 370).

The word "genus," then, is not understood by Marx in the sense of natural species, of a common naturalistic character inertly underpinning individual differences—and it is so little understood in this way that it is not a naturalistic connotation that founds man's character as *Gattungswesen*, but praxis, free and conscious activity. Rather, he understands it in the active sense of γένεσις συνεχής, that is, as the original principle (γένεσις) that in every individual and in every act founds man as a *human* being, and, thus founding him, con-tains him, holds him together with other men, makes of him a universal being.

In order to understand why Marx employs the word "genus" (*Gattung*) and why the characterization of man as being capable of genus holds pride of place in the development of his thought, we have to go back to Hegel's determination of genus in the *Phenomenology of Spirit*. Speaking of the value of genus in organic nature and of its relation to concrete individuality, Hegel says that the single living being is not at the same time a universal individual: the universality of organic life is purely contingent, and could be compared to a syllogism "where one of the extremes is life as universal or *genus*, and . . . the other, the same universal life, but as single and universal individual," but where the middle term, that is, the concrete individual, is not actually such since it does not contain in itself the two extremes between which it should mediate. Thus, unlike human consciousness, "organic nature," writes Hegel, "has no history; from its universal, namely life, it precipitates immediately into the singularity of the existing entity."

When the original unifying force of the Hegelian system dissolved, the problem of the reconciliation between "genus" and "individual," between the "concept of man" and "man in the flesh," occupied a crucial place in the meditations of the Young Hegelians, or left-wing Hegelians. The mediation of the individual and the genus was of particular interest to them because, by reconstituting man's universality on a concrete basis, it would have offered at the same time a solution to the problem of the unity of spirit and nature, of man as *natural* being and man as a human and *historical* being.

In a pamphlet published in 1845, which enjoyed much consideration in the circles of German socialism, Moses Hess described as follows the attempt (and failure) of the "last philosophers" (Stirner and Bauer) to reconcile the two opposed terms of Hegel's syllogism:

> It would occur to no one to affirm that the astronomer is the solar system of which he has become knowledgeable. However, the individual man who has acquired knowledge of nature and history should, according to our latest German philosophers, be the "genus" [*Gattung*], the "all." Each man, as one can read in Busch's journal, is the state, is humanity.—Each man is the genus, totality, humanity, the all, wrote the philosopher Julius recently.—"Just as the individual is the whole of nature, in the same way he is also the entire genus," says Stirner.
>
> Since the existence of Christianity people have been working to eliminate the difference between father and son, between divine and human, that is, between the "concept of man" and the "actual bodily" man. But just as Protestantism has not succeeded in this by suppressing the visible Church . . . , so too have the last philosophers, who have eliminated the invisible Church as well, yet have put in place of the heavens the "absolute Spirit," "self-consciousness," and *Gattungswesen*.[13]

Marx's reproach to Feuerbach in the sixth thesis of the *Theses on Feuerbach* was precisely that he had failed to reconcile the sensuous individual with universality in general, and thus that he had thought both abstractly, conceiving being only as "genus" ("*Gattung*," in quotation marks), that is, as "internal, mute generality that connects *naturally* many individuals [*als innere, stumme, die vielen*

Individuen natürlich *verbindende Allgemeinheit*]." The middle term, which constitutes man's genus, understood not as inert and material generality but as γένεσις, original active principle, is for Marx praxis, productive human activity. In this sense, praxis constitutes man's genus. This means that the production that is done in it is also "man's self-production," that is, the eternally active and present act of origin (γένεσις) that constitutes and con-tains man in his genus and that at the same time founds the unity of man with nature, of man as natural being and man as *human* natural being.

In the productive act, then, man becomes suddenly situated in a dimension that is inaccessible to any naturalistic chronology, since it is man's essential origin. Freeing himself at once of God (as prime creator) and nature (understood as the All independent of man, of which he is part with the same claim as animals), man posits himself, in the productive act, as the origin and nature of man.[14] This act of origin, then, is also the original act and the foundation of history understood as the becoming nature, for man, of human essence and the becoming man of nature. As such, that is, as man's genus and self-production, history abolishes "the nature that precedes men's history, which no longer exists anywhere these days, except on some recently formed Australian atoll," and, also suppressing itself as history, as *other* of nature, it posits itself as the "true natural history of man" (*MEGA*, p. 409). And since history is synonymous with society, Marx can say that society (whose act of origin is praxis) "is the fulfilled essential unity of man with nature, the true resurrection of nature, naturalism attained by man and humanism attained by nature" (*MEGA*, p. 391). It is also because Marx thinks production in this original dimension and because he experiences man's alienation as the crucial event in man's destiny that Marx's determination of praxis attains an essential horizon of man's history, of the destiny of the being whose status on earth is a productive one. Yet, although he locates praxis in man's original dimension, Marx does not think the essence of production beyond the horizon of modern metaphysics. For if at this point we ask what endows praxis, human production, with its generic power, making of it the original container of man—if we ask, in other words, what the feature is that distinguishes praxis from the mere vital activity proper also to other animals—the answer Marx gives us refers us back to that metaphysics of will whose origin we found in the Aristotelian determination of πράξις as ὄρεξις and νοῦς πρακτικός.

Marx defines praxis with respect to the vital activity of other animals as follows: "Man makes of his vital activity itself the object of his *will* and his *consciousness*"; "*free* and *conscious* activity is man's generic characteristic." While the characteristic of consciousness is for Marx a derived one ("consciousness is from the start a social product"), the original essence of will has its root in man as a natural being, as a *living* being. The Aristotelian definition of man as ζῷον λόγον ἔχων, a living entity endowed with λόγος, or *animal rationale*, necessarily implied an interpretation of the living being (ζῷον), whose original characteristic Aristotle determined—for the living being called man—as ὄρεξις in the threefold meaning of longing, desire, and volition. In the same way, Marx's definition of man as *human* natural being implies an interpretation of man as *natural* being, as a *living* being.

Man's characteristic as a living being is, for Marx, longing or drive (*Trieb*) and passion (*Leidenschaft, Passion*). "As a natural being, as a living natural being, [man] is partly endowed with *natural forces* [*natürliche Kräften*], with *vital forces* [*Lebenskräften*], that is, he is an *active* [*tätiges*] natural being; and these forces exist in him as dispositions and faculties, as drives [*Triebe*]" (*MEGA*, p. 408); "man as objective, sensuous being is therefore *passive* [*leidendes*], and since he feels his suffering [*Leiden*], he is a *passionate* [*leidenschaftliches*] being. Passionality, passion [*die Leidenschaft, die Passion*] is the essential force of man that tends energetically toward its object" (*MEGA*, p. 409).

When the conscious character of praxis is degraded—in the *German Ideology*—to a derived characteristic, and understood as practical consciousness, νοῦς πρακτικός, or immediate relationship with the surrounding sensuous environment, it is will, determined naturalistically as drive and passion, that remains as the sole original characteristic of praxis. Man's productive activity is, at bottom, vital *force*, drive and energetic tension, passion. The essence of praxis, the genetic characteristic of man as a *human* and historical being, has thus retreated into a naturalistic connotation of man as *natural* being. The original container of the living being "man," of the living being who produces, is will. Human production is praxis. "Man produces universally."

4. "Art Is the Highest Task and the Truly Metaphysical Activity of Man"

The problem of art, as such, does not present itself within Nietzsche's thought because all his thought is thought of art. There is no such thing as Nietzsche's aesthetics because Nietzsche never thought of art starting from αἴσθησις, from the spectator's sensuous apprehension—and yet it is in Nietzsche's thought that the aesthetic idea of art as the *opus* of an *operari*, as a creative-formal principle, attains the furthest point of its metaphysical itinerary. And precisely because the nihilistic fate of Western art has sought itself most extremely in Nietzsche's thought, modern aesthetics as a whole is still far from an awareness of its object that would respond to the high standing Nietzsche's thought gave to art in the circle of the eternal recurrence and in the mode of the will to power.

This standing declares itself early in the development of his thought, namely, in the preface to the *Birth of Tragedy*, this book in which "everything is an omen." It reads: "art is the highest task and the truly metaphysical activity of man."[15]

Art—as metaphysical activity—constitutes the highest task of man. This phrase does not mean, for Nietzsche, that the production of works of art is, from a cultural and ethical perspective, man's noblest and most important activity. The appeal spoken by this phrase cannot be understood in its proper dimension if it is not placed in the horizon of the advent of that "uncanniest of all guests" of which Nietzsche writes: "I describe what is coming, what can no longer come differently: *the advent of nihilism*."[16] The "value" of art, then, cannot be appreciated unless one starts from the "devaluation of all values." This devaluation of all values—which constitutes the essence of nihilism—has two opposite meanings for Nietzsche.[17] There is a nihilism that corresponds to "an increased power of spirit" and to a vital enrichment (Nietzsche calls it "active nihilism") and a nihilism that is a sign of "decline" and an impoverishment of life ("passive nihilism").[18] To this duplicity of meanings corresponds an analogous opposition between an art that is born of a superabundance of life and an art that is born of the wish to take revenge on life. This distinction is expressed fully in the *Gay Science*, in the aphorism called "What Is Romanticism?"—a text that Nietzsche considered important enough to reproduce it a few years later, with a few revisions, in "Nietzsche Contra Wagner":

> Regarding all aesthetic values I now avail myself of this main distinction: I ask in every instance, "is it hunger or superabundance that has here become creative?" At first glance, another distinction may seem preferable—it is far more obvious—namely the question whether the desire to fix, to immortalize, the desire for *being* prompted creation, or the desire for destruction, for change, for future, for *becoming*. But both of these kinds of desire are seen to be ambiguous when one considers them more closely; they can be interpreted in accordance with the first scheme that is, as it seems to me, preferable. The desire for *destruction*, change, and becoming can be an expression of an overflowing energy that is pregnant with future (my term for this is, as is known, "Dionysian"); but it can also be the hatred of the ill-constituted, disinherited, and underprivileged, who destroy, *must* destroy, because what exists, indeed all existence, all being, outrages and provokes them. To understand this feeling, consider our anarchists closely.
>
> The will to *immortalize* also requires a dual interpretation. It can be prompted, first, by gratitude and love; art with this origin will always be an art of apotheoses, perhaps dithyrambic like Rubens, or blissfully mocking like Hafiz, or bright and gracious like Goethe, spreading a Homeric light and glory over all things. But it can also be the tyrannical will of one who suffers deeply, who struggles, is tormented, and would like to turn what is most personal, singular, and narrow, the real idiosyncrasy of his suffering, into a binding law and compulsion—one who, as it were, revenges himself on all things by forcing his own image, the image of his torture, on them, branding them with it. This last version is *romantic pessimism* in its most expressive form, whether

it be Schopenhauer's philosophy of will or Wagner's music—romantic pessimism, the last *great* event in the fate of our culture.

(That there still *could* be an altogether different kind of pessimism, a classical type—this premonition and vision belongs to me as inseparable from me, as my *proprium* and *ipsissimum*; only the word "classical" offends my ears, it is far too trite and has become round and indistinct. I call this pessimism of the future—for it comes! I see it coming! *Dionysian* pessimism.)[19]

Nietzsche recognized that art—as negation and destruction of a world of truth opposed to a world of appearances—is tinged with nihilism as well; yet he interpreted this characteristic, at least for Dionysian art, as the expression of that active nihilism of which he would later write: "To this extent, nihilism, as the denial of a truthful world, of being, might be *a divine way of thinking*."[20]

In 1881, when he wrote *The Gay Science*, the process of distinction between art and passive nihilism (to which corresponds, in aphorism 370, romantic pessimism) was completed. "If we had not welcomed the arts and inverted this kind of cult of the untrue," he states,

> then the realization of general untruth and mendaciousness that now comes to us through science—the realization that delusion and error are conditions of human knowledge and sensation—would be utterly unbearable. *Honesty* would lead to nausea and suicide. But now there is a counterforce against our honesty that helps us to avoid such consequences: art as the *good* will to appearance. . . . As an aesthetic phenomenon existence is still *bearable* to us, and art furnishes us with eyes and hands and above all the good conscience to be *able* to turn ourselves into such a phenomenon.[21]

Understood in this dimension, art is "the only superior counterforce to all will to annihilation of life, the anti-Christian, anti-Buddhist, antinihilist *par excellence*."[22]

The word "art" here designates something incomparably broader than what we usually understand by this term, and its proper meaning will remain unattainable so long as we obstinately remain on the plane of aesthetics and aestheticism (this being the current interpretation of Nietzsche's thought). The dimension in which Nietzsche locates this highest metaphysical task of man is revealed by an aphorism called "Let Us Beware." If we tune our minds to the resonance proper to this aphorism, if we hear in it the voice of the one who teaches the eternal recurrence of the same, it will open for us a region in which art, will to power and eternal recurrence belong to one another reciprocally in one circle:

Let us beware.—Let us beware of thinking that the world is a living being. Where should it expand? On what should it feed? How could it grow and multiply? We have some notion of the nature of the organic; and we should not reinterpret the exceedingly derivative, late, rare, accidental, that we perceive only on the crust of the earth and make of it something essential, universal, and eternal, which is what those people do who call the universe an organism. This nauseates me. Let us even beware of believing that the universe is a machine: it is certainly not constructed for one purpose, and calling it a "machine" does it far too much honor.

Let us beware of positing generally and everywhere anything as elegant as the cyclical movements of our neighboring stars; even a glance into the Milky Way raises doubts whether there are not far coarser and more contradictory movements there, as well as stars with eternally linear paths, etc. The astral order in which we live is an exception; this order and the relative duration that depends on it have again made possible an exception of exceptions: the formation of the organic. The total character of the world, however, is in all eternity chaos—in the sense not of a lack of necessity but of a lack of order, arrangement, form, beauty, wisdom, and whatever other names there are for our aesthetic anthropomorphisms. Judged from the point of view of our reason, unsuccessful attempts are by all odds the rule, the exceptions are not the secret aim, and the whole musical box repeats eternally its tune which may never be called a melody—and ultimately even the phrase "unsuccessful attempt" is too anthropomorphic and reproachful. But how could we reproach or praise the universe? Let us beware of attributing to it heartlessness and unreason or their opposites: it is neither perfect nor beautiful, nor noble, nor does it wish to become any of these things; it does not by any means strive to imitate man. None of our aesthetic and moral judgments apply to it. Nor does it have any instinct for self-preservation or any other instinct; and it does not ob-

serve any laws either. Let us beware of saying that there are laws in nature. There are only necessities: there is nobody who commands, nobody who obeys, nobody who trespasses. Once you know that there
are no purposes, you also know that there is no accident; for it is only
beside a world of purposes that the word "accident" has meaning. Let
us beware of saying that death is opposed to life. The living is merely
a type of what is dead, and a very rare type.

Let us beware of thinking that the world eternally creates new
things. There are no eternally enduring substances; matter is as much
of an error as the God of the Eleatics. But when shall we ever be done
with our caution and care? When will all these shadows of God cease
to darken our minds? When will we complete our de-deification of nature? When may we begin to "*naturalize*" humanity in terms of a pure,
newly discovered, newly redeemed nature?[23]

We commonly understand "chaos" as that which by definition
lacks sense, the senseless as such. That the total character of the
world is for all eternity chaos means that all representations and
idealizations of our knowledge lose their meaning. Understood
within the horizon of the ascent of nihilism, this sentence means:
existence and world have neither value nor purpose, and all values
are devalued.

"The categories *purpose, unity, being,* with which we have attributed value to the world, have been taken away from us again,"
Nietzsche writes in the *Will to Power.* And yet, that the total character of the world is chaos does not mean for Nietzsche that it lacks
necessity; on the contrary, the aphorism from the *Gay Science* says
precisely that "there are only necessities." Purposelessness and sense-
lessness, however, are necessary: chaos is fate. In the conception of
chaos as necessity and fate, nihilism reaches its extreme form, that
in which it opens up to the idea of eternal recurrence: "Let us think
this thought in its most terrible form: existence as it is, without
meaning or aim, yet recurring inevitably without any finale of
nothingness: '*the eternal recurrence.*' This is the most extreme form
of nihilism: the nothing (the 'meaningless'), eternally!"[24]

In the idea of the eternal recurrence, nihilism attains its most extreme form, but precisely for this reason it enters a zone in which

surpassing it becomes possible. *Accomplished* nihilism and Zarathustra's message on the eternal recurrence of the same are part of
the same enigma, but are separated by an abyss. Their relationship—their closeness and, at the same time, their incommensu-
rable distance—is expressed by Nietzsche in the "Zarathustra"
chapter of *Ecce Homo*:

> The psychological problem in the type of Zarathustra is how he, who
> to an unheard-of degree says No, *does* No to everything to which one
> has hitherto said Yes, can none the less be the opposite of a spirit of
> denial; how he, a spirit bearing the heaviest of destinies, a fatality of a
> task, can none the less be the lightest and most opposite—Zarathustra
> is a dancer—: how he, who has the harshest, the most fearful insight
> into reality, who has thought the "most abysmal thought," none the
> less finds in it no objection to existence, nor even to the eternal recur-
> rence of existence—rather one more reason *to be himself* the eternal
> Yes to all things, "the tremendous unbounded Yes and Amen."[25]

An aphorism that opens the fourth book of *The Gay Science* shows
in what dimension this psychological knot is undone: "I want to
learn more and more to see as beautiful what is necessary in things;
then I shall be one of those who make things beautiful. *Amor fati*:
let that be my love henceforth . . . some day I wish to be only a
Yes-sayer."[26]

The essence of love for Nietzsche is will. *Amor fati* means: will
that what exists be what is, will of the circle of the eternal recurrence as *circulus vitiosus deus*. In the *amor fati*, in the will that wants
what is to the point of wishing its eternal recurrence and that, car-
rying the greatest burden, says yes to chaos and no longer wants
the eternal seal of becoming, nihilism reverses into extreme approbation of life:

> What, if some day or night a demon were to steal after you into your
> loneliest loneliness and say to you: "This life as you now live it and
> have lived it, you have to live once more and innumerable times more;
> and there will be nothing new in it, but every pain and every joy and
> every thought and sigh and everything unutterably small or great in
> your life will have to return to you, all in the same succession and se-

quence—even this spider and this moonlight between the trees, and even this moment and I myself. The eternal hourglass of existence is turned upside down again and again, and you with it, speck of dust!"

Would you not throw yourself down and gnash your teeth and curse the demon who spoke thus? Or have you once experienced a tremendous moment when you would have answered him: "You are a god and never have I heard anything more divine." If this thought gained possession of you, it would change you as you are or perhaps crush you. The question in each and every thing, "Do you desire this once more and innumerable times more?" would lie upon your actions as the greatest weight. Or how well disposed would you have to become to yourself and to life to *crave nothing more fervently* than this ultimate eternal confirmation and seal?[27]

Nihilism is surpassed in the man who recognizes his essence starting from this will and this love, and who tunes his being to the universal becoming in the circle of eternal recurrence. At the same time, chaos and nature are the object of a redemption that transforms every "it was" into "thus I wanted it to be." Will to power and eternal recurrence are not two ideas that Nietzsche casually places next to each other; they belong to the same origin and metaphysically mean the same thing. The expression "will to power" indicates the most intimate essence of being, understood as life and becoming, and the eternal recurrence of the same is the name of the "most extreme possible approximation of a world of becoming to a world of being." This is why Nietzsche can summarize in this form the essence of his thought: "Recapitulation: To impose upon becoming the character of being—that is the supreme will to power."[28]

Thought of in this metaphysical dimension, the will to power is the con-tainer of becoming, which traverses the circle of eternal recurrence and, traversing it, contains it; it transforms chaos into the "golden ball" of the great noonday, of the "hour of the shortest shadow" in which the advent of the superman is announced. Only within this horizon is it possible to understand what Nietzsche means when he affirms (in the preface to the *Birth of Tragedy*) that art "is the highest task of man, the true metaphysical activity."

Within the perspective of the surpassing of nihilism and the redemption of chaos, Nietzsche suddenly situates art outside any aesthetic dimension and thinks it within the circle of the eternal recurrence and of the will to power. In this circle, art presents itself to
Nietzsche's meditation as the fundamental trait of the will to
power, in which the essence of man and the essence of eternal becoming are identical to each other. Nietzsche calls *art* this standing of man within his metaphysical destiny. *Art* is the name he
gives to the essential trait of the will to power: the will that recognizes itself everywhere in the world and feels every event as the fundamental trait of its character is what is expressed, for Nietzsche,
in the value *art*.

The proof that Nietzsche thinks of art as the original metaphysical power, that his entire thought is, in this sense, a thought of art,
is in a fragment from the summer and fall of 1881: "We want to
have the experience of a work of art anew each time! Thus we must
mold life so as to have this same wish for each of its parts! This is
the main idea! Only at the end will the *theory* of the repetition of
everything that has existed be enunciated: only once the tendency
to create something that can *bloom* a hundred times better under
the sun of this theory has been inculcated!"[29] Only because he
thinks of art in this original dimension can Nietzsche say that "art
is *worth more* than truth" and that "we possess *art* lest we *perish of
the truth*."[30]

The man who takes on the "greatest burden" of the redemption
of nature is the man of art: the man who, starting from the ultimate tensions of the creative principle, has experienced in himself
the nothingness that demands a shape and has reversed this experience into extreme approbation of life, into adoration of appearance understood as "eternal joy of becoming, this joy that carries
in itself the joy of annihilation."

The man who accepts in his own will the will to power as the
fundamental trait of everything he is, and who wills himself starting from this will, is the superman. Superman and man of art are
the same thing. The hour of the shortest shadow, in which the difference between true world and world of appearances is abolished,

is also the blinding noonday of the "Olympus of appearances," of the world of art.

As the redemption of accident, the "highest task of man" points toward a becoming nature of art that is at the same time the becoming art of nature. In this extreme movement and in this nuptial union the ring of the eternal recurrence, the "golden ball" in which nature frees itself from the shadows of God and man naturalizes himself is tightened.

In a fragment from the last years, Nietzsche writes: "'*Without the Christian faith*,' Pascal thought, 'you, no less than nature and history, will become for yourselves *un monstre et un chaos*.' This prophecy we have fulfilled."[31] The man of art is that man who has fulfilled Pascal's prophecy and thus is "a monster and a chaos." But this monster and this chaos have the divine face and the halcyon smile of Dionysus, the god who reverses in his dance the most abyssal thought into the highest joy, and with whose name Nietzsche had, at the time of the *Birth of Tragedy*, already expressed the essence of art.

In his last year of intellectual lucidity, Nietzsche changed his mind about the title of the fourth book of the work that he was thinking of writing, *The Will to Power*. The projected titles now read: "Redemption of Nihilism"; "Dionysus, Philosophy of the Eternal Recurrence"; "Dionysus Philosopher." But in the essence of art, which has traversed its nothingness from end to end, it is will that reigns. Art is the eternal self-generation of the will to power. As such, it detaches itself both from the activity of the artist and from the sensibility of the spectator to posit itself as the fundamental trait of universal becoming. A fragment from the years 1885–86 reads: "The work of art where it appears without an artist, e.g., as body, as organism. . . . To what extent the artist is only a preliminary stage. The world as a work of art that gives birth to itself—"[32]

§ 9 The Original Structure of the Work of Art

"Everything is rhythm, the entire destiny of man is one heavenly rhythm, just as every work of art is one rhythm, and everything swings from the poetizing lips of the god."[1] This statement was not passed down to us by Hölderlin's own hand. It is from a period of his life—1807–43—that we usually define as the years of his insanity. The words that compose it were transcribed by a visitor's sympathetic hand from the "incoherent speech" that he uttered in his room in the house of the carpenter Zimmer. Bettina von Arnim, including them in her book *Die Günderode,* commented: "[Hölderlin's] words are for me like the words of an oracle, which he exclaims in his madness like the priest of the god, and certainly the whole worldly life is senseless for him, since it does not touch him. . . . He is an apparition, and light streams into my thought."[2]

What Hölderlin's sentence says appears at first blush too obscure and general to tempt us to take it into consideration in a philosophical query on the work of art. However, if we want to submit to its proper meaning, that is, if we want, in order to correspond to it, to make it first of all into a problem for us, then the question that immediately arises is: what is rhythm, which Hölderlin attributes to the work of art as its original characteristic?

The word "rhythm" is not foreign to the tradition of Western thought. We encounter it, for example, at a crucial point of Aristotle's *Physics,* at the beginning of Book II, precisely at the moment when Aristotle, after reviewing and criticizing the theories of his predecessors, tackles the problem of the definition of nature. To be sure, Aristotle does not directly use the word rhythm (ῥυθμός); however, he employs the privative expression τὸ ἀρρύθμιστον, meaning that which in itself lacks rhythm. Seeking the essence of nature, he relates the opinion of the sophist Antiphon, according to whom nature is τὸ πρῶτον ἀρρύθμιστον, that which is in itself shapeless and without structure, inarticulate matter subtended to any shape and mutation, that is, the prime and irreducible element (στοιχεῖον), identified by some with fire, by others with earth, air, and water (Aristotle, *Physics* 193a). In contrast to τὸ πρῶτον ἀρρύθμιστον, ῥυθμός is what adds itself to this immutable substratum and, by adding itself to it, composes and shapes it, giving it *structure*. In this sense, rhythm is *structure*, scheme, in opposition to elemental, inarticulate nature.³

Understood from this perspective, Hölderlin's sentence would mean that every work of art is one structure, and would therefore imply an interpretation of the original being of the work of art as ῥυθμός, structure. If this is true, the sentence would also in some way point toward the path taken by contemporary criticism when it seeks the "structures" of the work of art, abandoning traditional aesthetics.

But is it in fact so? Let us not rush to conclusions. If we look at the different meanings the word "structure" assumes today in the natural sciences, we notice that they all rotate around a definition derived from the psychology of form, which Lalande, in the second edition of his dictionary of philosophy, summarizes as follows: "in opposition to a simple combination of elements, a whole formed by phenomena in solidarity, such that each phenomenon depends on the others and can be what it is only in and through its relation with them."⁴ Structure then, like *Gestalt*, is a whole that contains something more than the simple sum of its parts.

If we now observe more closely the use that contemporary criticism makes of this word, we notice that there is in it a substantial ambiguity, such that "structure" designates sometimes the prime and irreducible element of the object in question, and sometimes what causes the ensemble to be what it is (that is, something more than the sum of its parts), in other words its proper status.

This ambiguity is not due to a simple imprecision or an arbitrariness on the part of the scholars who use the word "structure"; rather, it is the consequence of a difficulty already observed by Aristotle at the end of the seventh book of the *Metaphysics*. Here he asks what causes the fact that—in an ensemble that is not a mere aggregate (σωρός), but unity (ἕν, which corresponds to structure in the sense we have seen)—the whole is more than the simple combination of its elements: why, for instance, the syllable βα is not the consonant β plus the vowel α, but something else, ἕτερόν τι. Aristotle observes that the only solution that seems possible at first blush is that this "something else" is, in its turn, something other than an element or an ensemble constituted by elements. However, if this is true—as seems obvious, because this "something else" must exist in some way—the solution to the problem infinitely recedes (εἰς ἄπειρον βαδιεῖται), because the ensemble will now be the result of its parts *plus* another element, and the problem becomes that of the interminable search for an ultimate, irreducible element, beyond which it is not possible to proceed.

This was precisely the case for those thinkers who determined the character of nature as τὸ πρῶτον ἀρρύθμιστον and then looked for the prime elements (στοιχεῖα). It was in particular the case for the Pythagoreans: numbers (ἀριθμοί), because of their particular nature, at once material and immaterial, seemed to be the prime elements, and it was impossible to go back past them; thus the Pythagoreans thought that numbers were the original principles of all things. Aristotle's reproach to them was that they considered numbers at once as an element, that is, as the ultimate component, minimum *quantum*, and also as that which causes something to be what it is, as the original principle of the presence of an ensemble (*Metaphysics* i, 990a).

For Aristotle, the "something else" that causes the whole to be more than the sum of its parts had to be something radically other, that is, not an element that existed in the same way as the others— even if it were a prime, more universal element—but something that could be found only by abandoning the terrain of division ad infinitum to enter a more essential dimension. Aristotle designates this dimension as the αἰτία τοῦ εἶναι, the "cause of being," and the οὐσία, the principle that gives origin and maintains every thing in presence: not a material element but Form (μορφὴ καὶ εἶδος).

Therefore, in the passage from the second book of the *Physics* referred to earlier, Aristotle refuses the theory expounded by Antiphon and by all those who define nature as elementary matter, τὸ ἀρρύθμιστον, and instead identifies nature, that is, the original principle of presence, precisely with ῥυθμός, structure understood as synonymous with Form.

If we now ask again about the ambiguity of the term "structure" in the sciences of man, we see that in a way they make the same mistake that Aristotle attributed to the Pythagoreans. They start from the idea of structure as a whole that contains something more than its elements, but then—precisely to the extent that they intend to construct themselves as "sciences" by abandoning the region of philosophical inquiry—they understand this "something" as an *element* in its turn: the prime element, the ultimate *quantum* beyond which the object loses its reality. And since, as had already happened for the Pythagoreans, mathematics seems to offer a way to escape infinite regression, structural analysis seeks everywhere the original cipher (ἀριθμός) of the phenomenon that is its object, and tends more and more to adopt a mathematical method, thus joining that general process of mathematization of human concerns that is one of the essential characteristics of our time.[5]

Structural analysis, then, understands structure not only as ῥυθμός but also as number and elementary principle, that is, as precisely the opposite of a structure in the sense that the Greeks gave to this word. The search for structure in criticism and linguistics paradoxically corresponds to the obscuring and fading into the background of structure in its original meaning.

In structuralist research, then, there takes place a phenomenon analogous to that which took place in contemporary physics after the introduction of the notion of quantum action, because of which it is no longer possible to know at the same time the position of a corpuscle (the "figure," as Descartes said, in an expression corresponding to the Greek σχῆμα) and the amount of its movement. Structure in the sense of ῥυθμός and structure in the sense of ἀριθμός are two quantities traditionally conjugated in the sense that this expression assumes in contemporary physics, according to which it is not possible to know both at once. Hence the necessity to adopt statistical and mathematical methods, as in quantum physics: methods that make it possible to connect in a unitary representation the two conjugated quantities.

However, at least where the adoption of an exclusively mathematical method is impossible, structuralist inquiry remains condemned to oscillate endlessly between the two contradictory semantic poles of the term "structure": structure as *rhythm*, as that which causes something to be what it is, and structure as *number*, element and minimal *quantum*. Thus, to the extent that structuralist criticism asks about the work of art, the aesthetic idea of form is the ultimate obstacle that it can elude but not overcome, since it remains dependent on the aesthetic-metaphysical determination of the work of art as matter and form, and therefore represents the work of art at once as the object of an αἴσθησις and as original principle.

If rhythm and number are two opposite realities, then Hölderlin's statement cannot point toward the region inhabited by modern structuralist criticism. Rhythm is not structure in the sense of ἀριθμός, minimal *quantum*, and πρῶτον στοιχεῖον, primordial element, but is instead οὐσία, the principle of presence that opens and maintains the work of art in its original space. As such it is neither calculable nor rational; yet it is also not irrational, at least in the purely negative meaning this word is commonly understood to have. On the contrary, precisely because rhythm is that which causes the work of art to be what it is, it is also Measure and *logos* (*ratio*) in the Greek sense of that which gives every thing its proper station in presence. Rhythm attains this essential dimension, and is Measure in this original meaning; only for this reason is it able to open a region to human experience in which it can be perceived as ἀριθμός and *numerus*, as calculable measure expressible in number.

It is only because rhythm situates itself in a dimension in which the very essence of the work of art is at stake that the ambiguity is possible in which the work of art presents itself on the one hand as rational and necessary structure and on the other as pure, disinterested play, in a space in which calculation and play appear to blur into each other.

But what, then, is the essence of rhythm? What is the power that grants the work of art its original space? The word "rhythm" comes from the Greek ῥέω, to flow, as in the case of water. That which flows does so in a temporal dimension: it flows in time. According to a popular representation, time is nothing but pure flow, the incessant sequence of instants along an infinite line. As early a figure as Aristotle, thinking of time as ἀριθμός κινήσεος, the number of movement, and interpreting the instant as point (στίγμη), situated time in the one-dimensional region of an infinite numerical succession. This is the dimension of time that is familiar to us and that our chronometers measure with ever greater precision—whether they employ for this purpose the movement of cogwheels, as in common watches, or of weight and the radiation of matter, as in atomic chronometers.

Yet rhythm—as we commonly understand it—appears to introduce into this eternal flow a split and a stop. Thus in a musical piece, although it is somehow in time, we perceive rhythm as something that escapes the incessant flight of instants and appears almost as the presence of an atemporal dimension in time. In the same way, when we are before a work of art or a landscape bathed in the light of its own presence, we perceive a stop in time, as though we were suddenly thrown into a more original time. There is a stop, an interruption in the incessant flow of instants that, coming from the future, sinks into the past, and this interruption, this stop, is precisely what gives and reveals the particular status, the mode of presence proper to the work of art or the landscape we have before our eyes. We are as though held, arrested before something, but this being arrested is also a being-outside, an *ek-stasis* in a more original dimension.

Such reserve—which gives and at the same time hides its gift—

is called in Greek ἐποχή. The verb ἐπέχω, from which this word comes, has a double meaning: it means both to hold back, to suspend, and to hand over, to present, to offer. If we consider what we have just said about rhythm, that it reveals a more original dimension of time and at the same time conceals it in the one-dimensional flight of instants, we can perhaps, with only apparent violence, translate ἐποχή as rhythm, and say: rhythm is ἐποχή, gift and reserve. But the verb ἐπέχω has a third meaning in Greek, a meaning that unites in itself the other two: *to be*, in the sense of "to be present, to be there, to dominate, to hold." Thus the Greeks said ὁ ἄνεμος ἐπέχει, the wind *is*, that is: is present, dominates.

It is in this third sense that we should understand the verse of a poet who flourished at the time when Greek thought uttered its original word:

γίγνωσκε δ'οῖος ῥυθμός ἀνθρώπους ἔχει.

(Learn what Rhythm holds men.)[6]

Ὁ ῥυθμός ἔχει: rhythm holds, that is, gives and holds back, ἐπέχει. Rhythm grants men both the ecstatic dwelling in a more original dimension and the fall into the flight of measurable time. It holds *epochally* the essence of man, that is, gives him the gift both of being and of nothingness, both of the impulse in the free space of the work and of the impetus toward shadow and ruin. It is the original *ecstasy* that opens for man the space of his world, and only by starting from it can he experience freedom and alienation, historical consciousness and loss in time, truth and error.

Now, perhaps, we are able to understand in its proper meaning Hölderlin's sentence on the work of art. It points neither to an interpretation of the work of art as structure—that is, at once as *Gestalt* and number—nor to an exclusive attention to the stylistic unity of the work and its proper "rhythm," since both the structural and the stylistic analysis remain within the aesthetic conception of the work of art both as the (scientifically recognizable) object of αἴσθησις and as formal principle, *opus* of an *operari*. Instead, it points toward a determination of the original structure of the work of art as ἐποχή and rhythm, and thus situates it in a dimension in which the very structure of man's being-in-the-world and his relationship with truth and history are at stake. By opening to man his authentic temporal dimension, the work of art also opens for him the space of his belonging to the world, only within which he can take the original measure of his dwelling on earth and find again his present truth in the unstoppable flow of linear time.

In this authentic temporal dimension, the poetic status of man on earth finds its proper meaning. Man has on earth a poetic status, because it is *poiesis* that founds for him the original space of his world. Only because in the poetic ἐποχή he experiences his being-in-the-world as his essential condition does a world open up for his action and his existence. Only because he is capable of the most uncanny power, the power of pro-duction into presence, is he also capable of praxis, of willed and free activity. Only because he attains, in the poetic act, a more original temporal dimension is he a historical being, for whom, that is, at every instant his past and future are at stake.

Thus the gift of art is the most original gift, because it is the gift of the original site of man. The work of art is neither a cultural "value" nor a privileged object for the αἴσθησις of the spectators, nor the absolute creative power of the formal principle; instead it situates itself in a more essential dimension, because it allows man to attain his original status in history and time in his encounter with it. This is why Aristotle can say in the fifth book of the Metaphysics: ἀρχαὶ λέγονται καί αἱ τέχναι, καὶ τούτων αἱ ἀρχιτεκτονικαὶ μάλιστα, "arts are also called 'beginnings,' and of these especially the architectonic arts" (*Metaphysics* V, 1013a).

That art is architectonic means, etymologically: art, *poiesis*, is pro-duction (τίκτω) of origin (ἀρχή), art is the gift of the original space of man, *architectonics* par excellence. Just as all other mythic-traditional systems celebrate rituals and festivals to interrupt the homogeneity of profane time and, reactualizing the original mythic time, to allow man to become again the contemporary of the gods and to reattain the primordial dimension of creation, so in the work of art the *continuum* of linear time is broken, and man recovers, between past and future, his present space.

To look at a work of art, therefore, means to be hurled out into a more original time: it means ecstasy in the epochal opening of rhythm, which gives and holds back. Only by starting from this situation of man's relationship with the work of art is it possible to comprehend how this relationship—if it is authentic—is also for man the highest engagement, that is, the engagement that keeps him in the truth and grants to his dwelling on earth its original status. In the experience of the work of art, man stands in the truth, that is, in the origin that has revealed itself to him in the poietic act. In this engagement, in this being-hurled-out into the ἐποχή of rhythm, artists and spectators recover their essential solidarity and their common ground.

When the work of art is instead offered for aesthetic enjoyment and its formal aspect is appreciated and analyzed, this still remains far from attaining the essential structure of the work, that is, the origin that gives itself in the work of art and remains reserved in it. Aesthetics, then, is unable to think of art according to its proper statute, and so long as man is prisoner of an aesthetic perspective, the essence of art remains closed to him.

This original structure of the work of art is now obscured. At the extreme point of its metaphysical destiny, art, now a nihilistic power, a "self-annihilating nothing," wanders in the desert of *terra aesthetica* and eternally circles the split that cuts through it. Its alienation is the fundamental alienation, since it points to the alienation of nothing less than man's original historical space. In the work of art man risks losing not simply a piece of cultural wealth, however precious, and not even the privileged expression of his creative energy: it is the very space of his world, in which and only in which he can find himself as man and as being capable of action and knowledge.

If this is true, when man has lost his poetic status he cannot simply reconstruct his measure elsewhere: "it may be that any other salvation than that which comes from *where the* danger is, is still within non-safety [*Unheil*]."[7] Whether and when art will again have the task of taking the original measure of man on earth is not, therefore, a subject on which one can make predictions; neither can we say whether *poiesis* will recover its proper status beyond the interminable twilight that covers the *terra aesthetica.* The only thing we can say is that art will not simply be able to leap beyond its shadow to climb over its destiny.

§ 10 The Melancholy Angel

"The quotations in my works are like robbers lying in ambush on the highway to attack the passerby with weapons drawn and rob him of his conviction."[1] Walter Benjamin, the author of this statement, was perhaps the first European intellectual to recognize the fundamental change that had taken place in the transmissibility of culture and in the new relation to the past that constituted the inevitable consequence of this change. The particular power of quotations arises, according to Benjamin, not from their ability to transmit that past and allow the reader to relive it but, on the contrary, from their capacity to "make a clean sweep, to expel from the context, to destroy."[2] Alienating by force a fragment of the past from its historical context, the quotation at once makes it lose its character of authentic testimony and invests it with an alienating power that constitutes its unmistakable aggressive force.[3] Benjamin, who for his entire life pursued the idea of writing a work made up exclusively of quotations, had understood that the authority invoked by the quotation is founded precisely on the destruction of the authority that is attributed to a certain text by its situation in the history of culture. Its truth content is a function of the uniqueness of its appearance, alienated from its living context in what Benjamin, in his "Theses on the Philosophy of History," defines as "une citation à l'ordre du jour" ("a quotation on the order of the day") on the day of the Last Judgment. The past can only be fixed

in the image that appears once and for all in the instant of its alienation, just as a memory appears suddenly, as in a flash, in a moment of danger.[4]

This particular way of entering into a relation with the past also
constitutes the foundation of the activity of a figure with which
Benjamin felt an instinctive affinity: that of the collector. The collector also "quotes" the object outside its context and in this way
destroys the order inside which it finds its value and meaning.
Whether it is a work of art or any simple commodity that he, with
an arbitrary gesture, elevates to the object of his passion, the collector takes on the task of transfiguring things, suddenly depriving
them both of their use value and of the ethical-social significance
with which tradition had endowed them.

The collector frees things from the "slavery of usefulness" in the
name of their authenticity, which alone legitimates their inclusion
in the collection; yet this authenticity presupposes in turn the
alienation through which this act of freeing was able to take place,
by which the value for the connoisseur took the place of the use
value. In other words, the authenticity of the object measures its
alienation value, and this is in turn the only space in which the collection can sustain itself.[5]

Precisely because he makes alienation from the past into a value,
the figure of the collector is in some way related to that of the revolutionary, for whom the new can appear only through the destruction of the old. And it is certainly not an accident that the
great collector figures flourish precisely in times of break from tradition and exaltation of renewal: in a traditional society neither the
quotation nor the collection is conceivable, since it is not possible
to break at any point the links of the chain of tradition by which
the transmission of the past takes place.

It is peculiar that although Benjamin had observed the phenomenon through which the authority and the traditional value of
the work of art had begun to become unsteady, he nonetheless did
not notice that the "decline of the aura," as he sums up this
process, did not in any way effect the "freeing of the object from
its cultural sheath" and the subsequent founding of the object on

political praxis, but rather caused the reconstitution of a new "aura." Through this new aura, the object, re-creating and exalting to the utmost its authenticity on another level, became charged with a new value perfectly analogous to that alienation value that we have already observed with regard to the collection. Far from freeing the object from its authenticity, its technical reproducibility (which Benjamin identified as the main corrosive agent of the traditional authority of the work of art) carries authenticity to extremes: technical reproducibility is the moment when authenticity, by way of the multiplication of the original, becomes the very cipher of elusiveness.

This is to say: the work of art loses the authority and the guarantees it derived from belonging to a tradition for which it built the places and objects that incessantly weld past and present together. However, far from giving up its authenticity in order to become reproducible (thus fulfilling Hölderlin's wish that poetry might again become something that one could calculate and teach), the work of art instead becomes the locus of the most ineffable of mysteries, the epiphany of aesthetic beauty.

This phenomenon is particularly evident in Baudelaire, even though Benjamin considered him the poet in whom the decay of aura found its most typical expression. Baudelaire was the poet who had to face the dissolution of the authority of tradition in the new industrial society and therefore had to invent a new authority. He fulfilled this task by making the very intransmissibility of culture a new value and putting the experience of shock at the center of his artistic labor. The shock is the jolt power acquired by things when they lose their transmissibility and their comprehensibility within a given cultural order. Baudelaire understood that for art to survive the ruin of tradition, the artist had to attempt to reproduce in his work that very destruction of transmissibility that was at the origin of the experience of shock: in this way he would succeed in turning the work into the very vehicle of the intransmissible. Through the theorization of the beautiful as instantaneous and elusive epiphany (*un éclair ... puis la nuit!* ["a flash ... then night!"]), Baudelaire made of aesthetic beauty the cipher of the impossibility of transmission. We are now able to state more precisely what constitutes the alienation value that we have seen to be at the basis both of the quotation and of the activity of the collector, the alienation value whose production has become the specific task of the modern artist: it is nothing other than the destruction of the transmissibility of culture.

The reproduction of the dissolution of transmissibility in the experience of shock becomes, then, the last possible source of meaning and value for things themselves, and art becomes the last tie connecting man to his past. The survival of the past in the imponderable instant of aesthetic epiphany is, in the final analysis, the alienation effected by the work of art, and this alienation is in its turn nothing other than the measure of the destruction of its transmissibility, that is, of tradition.

∿

In a traditional system, culture exists only in the act of its transmission, that is, in the living act of its tradition. There is no discontinuity between past and present, between old and new, because every object transmits at every moment, without residue, the system of beliefs and notions that has found expression in it. To be more precise, in a system of this type it is not possible to speak of a culture independently of its transmission, because there is no accumulated treasure of ideas and precepts that constitute the separate object of transmission and whose reality is in itself a value. In a mythical-traditional system, an absolute identity exists between the act of transmission and the thing transmitted, in the sense that there is no other ethical, religious, or aesthetic value outside the act itself of transmission.

An inadequation, a gap between the act of transmission and the thing to be transmitted, and a valuing of the latter independently of the former appear only when tradition loses its vital force, and constitute the foundation of a characteristic phenomenon of non-traditional societies: the accumulation of culture. For, contrary to what one might think at first sight, the breaking of tradition does not at all mean the loss or devaluation of the past: it is, rather, likely that only now the past can reveal itself with a weight and an influence it never had before. Loss of tradition means that the past has lost its transmissibility, and so long as no new way has been found to enter into a relation with it, it can only be the object of accumulation from now on. In this situation, then, man keeps his cultural heritage in its totality, and in fact the value of this heritage multiplies vertiginously. However, he loses the possibility of drawing from this heritage the criterion of his actions and his welfare and thus the only concrete place in which he is able, by asking about his origins and his destiny, to found the present as the relationship between past and future. For it is the transmissibility of culture that, by endowing culture with an immediately perceptible meaning and value, allows man to move freely toward the future without being hindered by the burden of the past. But when a culture loses its means of transmission, man is deprived of reference points and finds himself wedged between, on the one hand, a past that incessantly accumulates behind him and oppresses him with the multiplicity of its now-indecipherable contents, and on the other hand a future that he does not yet possess and that does not throw any light on his struggle with the past. The interruption of tradition, which is for us now a *fait accompli*, opens an era in which no link is possible between old and new, if not the infinite accumulation of the old in a sort of monstrous archive or the alienation effected by the very means that is supposed to help with the transmission of the old. Like the castle in Kafka's novel, which burdens the village with the obscurity of its decrees and the multiplicity of its offices, the accumulated culture has lost its living meaning and hangs over man like a threat in which he can in no way recognize himself. Suspended in the void between old and new, past and future, man is projected into time as into something alien that incessantly eludes him and still drags him forward, but without allowing him to find his ground in it.

~

In the "Theses on the Philosophy of History," Benjamin employs a particularly felicitous image to describe this situation of the man who has lost his link with his past and is no longer able to find himself in history:

> A Klee painting named "Angelus Novus" shows an angel looking as though he is about to move away from something he is fixedly contemplating. His eyes are staring, his mouth is open, his wings are spread. This is how one pictures the angel of history. His face is turned toward the past. Where we perceive a chain of events, he sees one single catastrophe which keeps piling wreckage upon wreckage and hurls it in front of his feet. The angel would like to stay, awaken the dead, and make whole what has been smashed. But a storm is blowing from Paradise; it has got caught in his wings with such violence that the angel can no longer close them. This storm irresistibly propels him into the future to which his back is turned, while the pile of debris before him grows skyward. This storm is what we call progress.[6]

There is a well-known engraving by Dürer that presents some analogies with Benjamin's interpretation of Klee's painting. It represents a winged creature in a sitting position, in the act of meditating while looking ahead with an absorbed expression. Next to it, abandoned, the utensils of active life lie on the ground: a grindstone, a plane, nails, a hammer, a framing square, a pair of pincers, and a saw. The beautiful face of the angel is in the shadow; the light is reflected only by his long robe and a sphere set in front of his feet. Behind him we see an hourglass (the sand is flowing), a bell, a set of scales, and a magic square, and then, over the sea in the background, a comet shining without any brightness. A twilight atmosphere is diffused over the entire scene; it deprives every detail of materiality.

If Klee's *Angelus Novus* is the angel of history, nothing could represent the angel of art better than the winged creature in Dürer's engraving. While the angel of history looks toward the past, yet cannot stop his incessant flight backward toward the future, so the melancholy angel in Dürer's engraving gazes unmovingly ahead. The storm of progress that has gotten caught in that angel's wings has subsided here, and the angel of art appears immersed in an atemporal dimension, as though something, interrupting the continuum of history, had frozen the surrounding reality in a kind of messianic arrest. However, just as the events of the past appear to the angel of history as a pile of indecipherable ruins, so the utensils of active life and the other objects scattered around the melancholy angel have lost the significance that their daily usefulness endowed them with and have become charged with a potential for alienation that transforms them into the cipher for something endlessly elusive. The past that the angel of history is no longer able to comprehend reconstitutes its form in front of the angel of art; but this form is the alienated image in which the past finds its truth again only on condition of negating it, and knowledge of the new is possible only in the nontruth of the old. The redemption that the angel of art offers to the past, summoning it to appear outside its real context on the day of aesthetic Last Judgment, is, then, nothing other than its death (or rather, its inability to die) in the museum of aesthetics. And the angel's melancholy is the consciousness that he has adopted alienation as his world; it is the nostalgia of a reality that he can possess only by making it unreal.[7]

Aesthetics, then, in a way performs the same task that tradition performed before its interruption: knotting up again the broken thread in the plot of the past, it resolves the conflict between old and new without whose settlement man, this being that has lost himself in time and must find himself again, and for whom therefore at every instant his past and future are at stake, is unable to live. By destroying the transmissibility of the past, aesthetics recuperates it negatively and makes intransmissibility a value in itself in the image of aesthetic beauty, in this way opening for man a space between past and future in which he can found his action and his knowledge.

This space is the aesthetic space, but what is transmitted in it is precisely the impossibility of transmission, and its truth is the negation of the truth of its contents. A culture that in losing its transmissibility has lost the sole guarantee of its truth and become threatened by the incessant accumulation of its nonsense now relies on art for its guarantee; art is thus forced to guarantee something that can only be guaranteed if art itself loses its guarantees in turn.

The humble activity of the τεχνίτης who, by opening for man the space of work, built the places and objects in which tradition accomplished its incessant process of welding past to present, now leaves its place to the creative activity of the genius who is burdened with the imperative to produce beauty. In this sense one can say that on the one hand, kitsch, which considers beauty as the immediate goal of the work of art, is the specific product of aesthetics, while on the other hand, the ghost of beauty that kitsch evokes in the work of art is nothing but the destruction of the transmissibility of culture, in which aesthetics is founded.

If the work of art is the place in which the old and the new have to resolve their conflict in the present space of truth, the problem of the work of art and of its destiny in our time is not simply a problem among the others that trouble our culture: not because art occupies an elevated station in the (disintegrating) hierarchy of cultural values, but because what is at stake here is the very survival of culture, a culture split by a past and present conflict that has found its extreme and precarious settlement in our society in the form of aesthetic alienation. Only the work of art ensures a phantasmagoric survival for the accumulated culture, just as only the indefatigable demystifying action of the land surveyor K. ensures for Count West-West's castle the sole appearance of reality it can lay claim to. But the castle of culture has now become a museum in which, on the one hand, the wealth of the past, in which man can in no way recognize himself, is accumulated to be offered to the aesthetic enjoyment of the members of the community, and, on the other, this enjoyment is possible only through the alienation that deprives it of its immediate meaning and of its poietic capacity to open its space to man's action and knowledge.

Thus aesthetics is not simply the privileged dimension that progress in the sensibility of Western man has reserved for the work of art as his most proper place; it is, rather, the very destiny of art in the era in which, with tradition now severed, man is no longer able to find, between past and future, the space of the present, and gets lost in the linear time of history. The angel of history, whose wings became caught in the storm of progress, and the

angel of aesthetics, who stares in an atemporal dimension at the ruins of the past, are inseparable. And so long as man has not found
another way to settle individually and collectively the conflict between old and new, thus appropriating his historicity, a surpassing
of aesthetics that would not be limited to exaggerating the split
that traverses it appears unlikely.

~

There is a note in Kafka's notebooks in which this inability of
man to recover his space in the tension between past and future
history is expressed with particular precision in the image of

> . . . travelers in a train that has met with an accident in a tunnel, and
> this at a place where the light of the beginning can no longer be seen,
> and the light of the end is so very small a glimmer that the gaze must
> continually search for it and is always losing it again, and, further-
> more, it is not even certain whether it is the beginning or the end of
> the tunnel.[8]

At the time of Greek tragedy, when the traditional mythic system had begun to decline under the impulse of the new moral
world that was being born, art had already assumed the task of set-
tling the conflict between old and new, and had responded to this
task with the figure of the guilty innocent, of the tragic hero who
expresses in all his greatness and misery the precarious significance
of human action in the interval between what is no longer and
what is not yet.

Kafka is the author of our time who has most coherently assumed this task. Faced with man's inability to appropriate his own
historical presuppositions, he tried to turn this impossibility into
the very soil on which man might recover himself. In order to realize this project, Kafka reversed Benjamin's image of the angel of
history: the angel has already arrived in Paradise—in fact he was
there from the start, and the storm and his subsequent flight along
the linear time of progress are nothing but an illusion he creates in
the attempt to falsify his knowledge and to transform his perennial
condition into an aim still to be attained.

It is in this sense that the apparently paradoxical thought expressed in the "Reflections on Sin, Pain, Hope, and the True Way" should be understood: "There is a goal, but no path; what we call the path is only wavering," and "Only our concept of Time makes it possible for us to call the day of the Last Judgment by that name; in reality it is a summary court in perpetual session [*Standrecht*]."⁹ For man it is always already the day of the Last Judgment: the Last Judgment is his normal historical condition, and only his fear of facing it creates the illusion that it is still to come. Kafka thus replaces the idea of a history infinitely unfolding along an empty, linear time (this is the history that compels the *Angelus Novus* to his unstoppable run) with the paradoxical image of a *state of history* in which the fundamental event of the human condition is perpetually taking place; the continuum of linear time is interrupted, but does not create an opening beyond itself.¹⁰ The goal is inaccessible not because it is too far in the future but because it is present here in front of us; but its presence is constitutive of man's historicity, of his perennial lingering along a nonexistent path, and of his inability to appropriate his own historical situation.

This is why Kafka can say that the revolutionary movements that declare null and void everything that has happened before are right, because in reality nothing has happened yet. The condition of man who has gotten lost in history ends up looking like that of the southern Chinese in the story told in *The Great Wall of China*: "There is also involved a certain feebleness of faith and imaginative power on the part of the people, that prevents them from raising the empire out of its stagnation in Peking and clasping it in all its palpable living reality to their own breasts, which yet desire nothing better than but once to feel that touch and then to die." And yet "this very weakness should seem to be one of the greatest unifying influences among our people; indeed, if one may dare to use the expression, the very ground on which we live."¹¹

In the face of this paradoxical situation, asking about art's task is the equivalent of asking what could be its task on the day of the Last Judgment, that is, in a condition (which for Kafka is man's very historical status) in which the angel of history has stopped and, in the interval between past and future, man has to face his own responsibility. Kafka answered this question by asking whether art could become transmission of the act of transmission: whether, that is, it could take as its content the task of transmission itself, independently of the thing to be transmitted. As Benjamin understood, Kafka's genius before the unprecedented historical situation of which he had become aware was that he "sacrificed truth for the sake of transmissibility."[12] Since the goal is already present and thus no path exists that could lead there, only the perennially late stubbornness of a messenger whose message is nothing other than the task of transmission can give back to man, who has lost his ability to appropriate his historical space, the concrete space of his action and knowledge.

In this way, at the limit of its aesthetic itinerary, art abolishes the gap between the thing to be transmitted and the act of transmission and again comes closer to the mythic-traditional system, in which a perfect identity existed between the two terms. In this "attack on the last earthly frontier,"[13] art transcends the aesthetic dimension and thus, with the construction of a totally abstract moral system, eludes the fate that destined it to kitsch. Yet, although it can reach the threshold of myth, it cannot cross it. If man could appropriate his historical condition, and if, seeing through the illusion of the storm that perennially pushes him along the infinite rail of linear time, he could exit his paradoxical situation, he would at the same time gain access to the total knowledge capable of giving life to a new cosmogony and to turn history into myth. But art alone cannot do this, since it is precisely in order to reconcile the historical conflict between past and future that it has emancipated itself from myth and linked itself to history.

By transforming the principle of man's delay before truth into a poetic process and renouncing the guarantees of truth for love of transmissibility, art succeeds once again in transforming man's inability to exit his historical status, perennially suspended in the inter-world between old and new, past and future, into the very space in which he can take the original measure of his dwelling in the present and recover each time the meaning of his action.

According to the principle by which it is only in the burning house that the fundamental architectural problem becomes visible for the first time, art, at the furthest point of its destiny, makes visible its original project.

Reference Matter

Notes

1. The Most Uncanny Thing

1. Friedrich Nietzsche, *On the Genealogy of Morals*, trans. Walter Kaufmann (New York: Vintage Books, 1967), pp. 104–5.

2. Antonin Artaud, *Theater and Its Double*, trans. Mary Carolin Richards (New York: Grove Press, 1958), pp. 10–11. All further translations of *Le théâtre et son double* are modified from this edition.

3. Plato, *Republic*, trans. Paul Shorey, Loeb Classical Library (Cambridge, Mass.: Harvard University Press, 1953), I, 398a (1: 243–45), and II, 607a (2: 464–65). (This edition will henceforth be cited as "Shorey.") Plato writes "if a man capable of assuming every kind of shape and imitating all things . . . " because his target in the *Republic* is mimetic poetry (the poetry, namely, that by imitating passions attempts to evoke the same passions in the soul of the listeners) and not simply narrative poetry (διήγησις). It is not possible to understand the grounds for Plato's often-discussed opposition to the poets if one does not reconnect it to a theory of the relationship between language and violence. Its presupposition is the discovery that the principle—which in Greece had been tacitly held to be true until the rise of sophistics—according to which language excluded from itself any possibility of violence was no longer valid, and that in fact the use of violence was an integral part of poetic language. Once this discovery was made, it was perfectly consistent on Plato's part to establish that the genres (and even the rhythms and meters) of poetry must be overseen by the custodians of the State.

It is interesting to note that the introduction of violence into language, observed by Plato at the time of the so-called "Greek Enlightenment," is again observed (and even consciously planned by the libertine writers) at the end of the eighteenth century, simultaneously with modern Enlightenment, as though the intention of "enlightening" minds and the affirmation of freedom of opinion and speech were inseparable from the recourse to linguistic violence.

4. Sophocles, *Antigone*, trans. Elizabeth Wyckoff, in *Three Tragedies* (Chicago: University of Chicago Press, 1954), ll. 372–37, p. 171. For the interpretation of the first chorus of the *Antigone*, see Martin Heidegger, *An Introduction to Metaphysics*, trans. Ralph Manheim (New Haven, Conn.: Yale University Press, 1959), pp. 146–65.

5. See Edgar Wind, *Art and Anarchy* (New York: Knopf, 1964), p. 9.

6. Friedrich Nietzsche, *Human, All Too Human*, trans. Marion Faber, with Stephen Lehmann (Lincoln: University of Nebraska Press, 1984), aphorism 212, p. 127.

7. Plato, *Republic* II, 607c; Shorey, 2: 466–67.

8. Friedrich Hölderlin, letters to Casmir Ulrich Böhlendorff no. 236 (December 4, 1801) and no. 240 (November 1802?), in *Essays and Letters on Theory*, trans. Thomas Pfau (Albany: State University of New York Press, 1988), pp. 151, 152.

9. Friedrich Hölderlin, *Sämtliche Werke*, ed. Friedrich Beissner (Stuttgart: Cottasche Buchhandlung Nachfolger, 1943–85), 2: 228.

10. Friedrich Nietzsche, *The Gay Science: With a Prelude in Rhymes and an Appendix of Songs*, trans. Walter Kaufmann (New York: Vintage, 1974), p. 37. The first sentence is from a draft of the preface to the second edition of the book.

2. Frenhofer and His Double

1. See Martin Heidegger, "The Origin of the Work of Art," in *Poetry, Language, Thought*, trans. Albert Hofstadter (New York: Harper and Row, 1971), pp. 19–20: "The art work is, to be sure, a thing that is made, but it says something other than the mere thing itself is, *allo agoreuei*. The work makes public something other than itself; it manifests something other; it is an allegory. In the work of art something other is brought together with the thing that is made."

2. Degas, quoted in Paul Valéry, *Tel Quel*, in *Oeuvres*, ed. Jean Hytier, vol. 2 (Paris: Gallimard, 1960), p. 474. An analogous tendency toward what one could call the "dullness of the absolute" can also be found in

Baudelaire's aspiration to create a commonplace: "Créer un poncif, c'est le génie. Je dois créer un poncif." ["To create a cliché, that's genius. I must create a cliché."] Charles Baudelaire, *Fusées*, in *Oeuvres complètes*, ed. Claude Pichois, vol. 1 (Paris: Gallimard, 1975), p. 662.

3. Honoré de Balzac, *Le chef-d'oeuvre inconnu* (The unknown masterpiece), in *La comédie humaine* (Paris: Furne, 1845), 14: 300, 304, 306. Page references to this edition will be given in the text.

4. Maurice Blanchot, "The Sleep of Rimbaud," in *The Work of Fire*, trans. Charlotte Mandell (Stanford, Calif.: Stanford University Press, 1995), p. 154.

3. The Man of Taste and the Dialectic of the Split

1. [The word translated "split" in the title of this chapter and almost everywhere else in this book is *lacerazione*, which is in turn the Italian translation of Hegel's term *Zerrissenheit* in the passage quoted below from the *Phenomenology of Spirit*. A more literal translation would be "the state of being torn."—*Trans.*]

2. Jean de La Bruyère, *Characters*, trans. Henri Van Laun (New York: Oxford University Press, 1963), p. 2.

3. Paul Valéry, *Tel Quel*, in *Oeuvres*, ed. Jean Hytier, vol. 2 (Paris: Gallimard, 1960), p. 476.

4. Edgar Wind, *Art and Anarchy*, p. 91, quoting Lord Bridges, Romanes Lecture, Oxford, 1958. Even in the fifteenth century, the figure of the patron commissioning the work was still so tightly connected with the work of art that it would occur to very few artists to paint otherwise than on commission, simply on the strength of some inner necessity. Particularly tragic is the case of the Burgundian sculptor Claes van der Werve, who, because of the constant postponing of his project by Jean sans Peur, who had hired him, wasted in unproductive waiting an artistic career that had begun brilliantly. See Johann Huizinga, *The Waning of the Middle Ages*, trans. F. Hopman (New York: Doubleday, 1924), p. 254.

5. Jacob Burckhardt, *The Cicerone: An Art Guide to Painting in Italy*, trans. A. H. Clough (London, 1918; reprint, New York: Garland, 1979), p. 125.

6. Gustave Flaubert, *Bouvard and Pécuchet*, trans. A. J. Krailsheimer (Baltimore, Md.: Penguin, 1976), p. 294.

7. It has been jokingly observed that without the notion of the "great

artist" (that is, without the differentiation in quality that good taste makes among artists), there would have been fewer bad artists as well: "La notion de 'grand poète' a engendré plus de petits poètes qu'il n'en était raisonnablement à attendre des combinaisons du sort" ("the notion of the 'great poet' has engendered more small poets than one could have reasonably expected from the combinations of fate"). Valéry, *Tel Quel*, p. 487.

8. Voltaire, *Vie de Molière avec de petits sommaires de ses pièces*, ed. Hugues Pradier (Paris: Gallimard, 1992), p. 65.

9. Jean-Jacques Rousseau, *Letter to M. D'Alembert on the Theatre*, in *Politics and the Arts*, trans. Allan Bloom (Glencoe, Ill.: Free Press, 1960), p. 35.

10. Marie (de Rabutin Chantal) Sévigné, letter to Madame de Grignan, July 12, 1671, in *Lettres*, ed. Gérard-Gailly, vol. 1 (Paris: Gallimard, 1956), p. 332.

11. Pierre Moreau, "Les mystères Béranger," *Revue d'histoire littéraire de la France* 40 (1933): 197, quoted in Benedetto Croce, *La poesia*, 5th edition (Bari: Laterza, 1953), pp. 308–9.

12. Arthur Rimbaud, "Alchimie du verbe," *Une saison en enfer*, in *Oeuvres*, ed. Suzanne Bernard (Paris: Garnier, 1964), p. 228.

13. Friedrich Schlegel, *Lucinde*, in *Kritische Friedrich-Schlegel-Ausgabe*, ed. Hans Eichner, vol. 5 (Munich: Schöning, 1962), p. 28.

14. Denis Diderot, *Rameau's Nephew*, in *Rameau's Nephew and D'Alembert's Dream*, trans. Leonard Tancock (New York: Penguin, 1966), pp. 107–8.

15. Ibid., pp. 116–17.

16. G. W. F. Hegel, *Phenomenology of Spirit*, trans. A. V. Miller (New York: Oxford University Press, 1977), pp. 314–17.

17. Martin Heidegger, "The Word of Nietzsche: 'God is Dead,'" in *The Question Concerning Technology and Other Essays*, trans. William Lovitt (New York: Harper and Row, 1977), p. 62.

4. The Cabinet of Wonder

1. David Teniers, *Le théâtre des peintures de Davide Teniers* (Antwerp: n.p., 1673).

2. *La carta de navegar pittoresco, compartita in oto venti con i quali la Nave Venetiana viene conduita in l'alto mar de la Pitura* (Chart of pictor-

ial navigation, divided into eight winds by which the venetian ship is pushed on the high seas of painting) (Venice: n.p., 1660), seventh wind.

3. Johan Huizinga, *The Waning of the Middle Ages*, trans. F. Hopman (New York: Doubleday, 1924), p. 267.

4. G. W. F. Hegel, *Aesthetics: Lectures on Fine Art*, trans. T. M. Knox, vol. 1 (Oxford: Clarendon Press, 1975), p. 603.

5. Ibid., p. 605.

5. *"Les jugements sur la poésie"*

1. G. W. F. Hegel, *Aesthetics: Lectures on Fine Art*, trans. T. M. Knox, vol. 1 (Oxford: Clarendon Press, 1975), pp. 11, 13.

2. Immanuel Kant, *Critique of Judgment*, trans. J. H. Bernard (New York: Hafner, 1951), § 5, p. 45. Further references by paragraph and page number will be given in the text.

3. "The statues are now only stones from which the living soul has flown, just as the hymns are words from which belief has gone. The tables of the gods provide no spiritual food and drink, and in his games and festivals man no longer recovers the joyful consciousness of his unity with the divine. The works of the Muse now lack the power of the Spirit, for the Spirit has gained its certainty of itself from the crushing of gods and men. They have become what they are for us now—beautiful fruit already picked from the tree, which a friendly Fate has offered us, as a girl might set the fruit before us. It cannot give us the actual life in which they existed, not the tree that bore them, not the earth and the elements which constituted their substance, not the climate which gave them their peculiar character, nor the cycle of the changing seasons that governed the process of their growth. So Fate does not restore their world to us along with the works of antique Art, it gives not the spring and summer of the ethical life in which they blossomed and ripened, but only the veiled recollection of that actual world. Our active enjoyment of them is therefore not an act of divine worship through which our consciousness might come to its perfect truth and fulfillment; it is an external activity—the wiping-off of some drops of rain or specks of dust from these fruits, so to speak—one which erects an intricate scaffolding of the dead elements of their outward existence—the language, the historical circumstances, etc. in place of the inner elements of the ethical life which environed, created, and inspired them." G. W. F. Hegel, *Phenomenology*

of Spirit, trans. A. V. Miller (New York: Oxford University Press, 1977), pp. 455–56.

4. Benedetto Croce, *Estetica come scienza dell'espressione e linguistica generale* (Bari: Laterza, 1965), p. 32.

5. This observation can be found in the unfinished study on Sainte-Beuve that occupied Proust in the years immediately preceding the writing of the *Recherche du temps perdu.* See Marcel Proust, *Contre Sainte-Beuve* (Paris: Gallimard, 1954), p. 160.

6. Hegel, *Phenomenology of Spirit*, p. 316.

7. Arthur Rimbaud, letter to Georges Izambard, May 13, 1871: "Je est un autre. Tant pis pour le bois qui se trouve violon." ("I is another. So much the worse for the wood that finds itself to be a violin.") Letter to Paul Demeny, May 15, 1871: "Je est un autre. Si le cuivre s'éveille clairon . . . " ("I is another. If the brass wakes up as a bugle . . . "). Both letters are in Arthur Rimbaud, *Oeuvres*, ed. Suzanne Bernard (Paris: Garnier, 1964), pp. 344–45.

8. Robert Musil, "Schwarze Magie," in *Prosa und Stücke, Kleine Prosa, Aphorismen, Autobiographisches, Essays und Reden, Kritik*, ed. Adolf Frisé (Reinbeck bei Hamburg, Germany: Rowohlt, 1978), pp. 501, 503.

6. A Self-Annihilating Nothing

1. Plato, *Republic* II, 607b; Shorey, 2: 464–66. [Shorey's translation for the second quoted phrase, "the mob that masters those who are too wise for their own good," translates a reading of the Greek text as καὶ ὁ τῶν διασόφων ὄχλος κρατῶν. The edition of Plato from which Agamben is translating here has τῶν Δια σοφῶν instead. For alternative readings of the same passage, see James Adams's notes to his annotated edition of the *Republic*: Plato's *Republic*, ed. James Adam, 2d edition, introduction by D. A. Rees (Cambridge, Eng.: Cambridge University Press, 1963), 2: 418, 468, —*Trans.*]

2. G. W. F. Hegel, *Aesthetics: Lectures on Fine Art*, trans. T. M. Knox, vol. 1 (Oxford: Clarendon Press, 1975), pp. 9, 10, 11, 103).

3. Martin Heidegger, "The Origin of the Work of Art," in *Poetry, Language, Thought*, trans. Albert Hofstadter (New York: Harper and Row, 1971), p. 80.

4. Hegel, *Aesthetics* 1: 103, 607.

5. Charles Baudelaire, "De l'essence du rire et généralement du

comique dans les arts plastiques," in *Oeuvres complètes*, ed. Claude Pichois, vol. 2 (Paris: Gallimard, 1976), pp. 530, 543.

6. Ibid., p. 531.

7. Hegel, *Aesthetics*, 1: 67. [Knox translates "null in its self-destruction."]

8. Friedrich Nietzsche, *The Gay Science: With a Prelude in Rhymes and an Appendix of Songs*, trans. Walter Kaufmann (New York: Vintage, 1974), aphorism 125, p. 181.

9. Giovanni Urbani, in *Vacchi* (Catalogue of the exhibition) (Rome: n.p., 1962).

7. Privation Is Like a Face

1. Plato, *Symposium*, trans. Michael Joyce, in Plato, *The Collected Dialogues*, ed. Edith Hamilton and Huntington Cairns (Princeton, N.J.: Princeton University Press, 1961), 205b, p. 557.

2. We write "pro-duction" and "pro-duct" to indicate the essential character of ποίησις, that is, the pro-duction into presence; we write "production" and "product" to refer in particular to the doing of technology and industry.

3. See Aristotle, *Physics* 192 b. For an enlightening interpretation of the second book of this work, see Martin Heidegger, "Vom Wesen und Begriff der φύσις. Aristoteles' Physik B, I" (1939), now in *Wegmarken* (Frankfurt a.M.: Vittorio Klostermann, 1976), pp. 239–301.

4. Friedrich Hölderlin, "Remarks on 'Oedipus,'" in *Essays and Letters on Theory*, trans. and ed. Thomas Pfau (Albany: State University of New York Press, 1988), p. 101.

5. Aristotle, *Physics*, trans. R. P. Hardie and R. K. Gaye, in *The Basic Works of Aristotle*, ed. Richard McKeon (New York: Random House, 1941), 193a, pp. 237–38.

8. Poiesis and Praxis

1. See Hannah Arendt, *The Human Condition* (Chicago: University of Chicago Press, 1958), chap. 1. The distinction between work (as in the work of art), action, and work (as in labor) is the center of the analysis of *vita activa* performed by the author.

2. See ibid., chap. 3.

3. Friedrich Hardenberg (Novalis), *Werke, Briefe, Dokumente*, ed.

Ewald Wasmuth, vol. 2 (Heidelberg: Lambert Schneider, 1957), frag. 1339. Henceforth cited in text by fragment number.

4. The definition that Aristotle, in the *Nicomachean Ethics*, gives of τέχνη as ἕξις ποιητική says—if understood correctly—nothing different. The usual translation of εξις ποιητική is "productive quality or habit." But ἕξις is, properly, a species of θέσις, more precisely a διάθεσις, a disposition or attitude. Thus ἕξις ποιητική means productive disposition.

5. Aristotle, *Nicomachean Ethics*, trans. W. D. Ross, in *The Basic Works of Aristotle*, ed. Richard McKeon (New York: Random House, 1941), VI, 1140b, p. 1026.

6. Aristotle, *Metaphysics*, trans. W. D. Ross, in *Basic Works*, I, 981a, pp. 690–91.

7. Ibid., p. 689.

8. Ibid. II, 993b, p. 712.

9. Aristotle, *De anima*, trans. J. A. Smith, in *Basic Works*, 433a, p. 598.

10. Friedrich Wilhelm Joseph von Schelling, *Of Human Freedom*, trans. James Gutmann (Chicago: Open Court, [1936]), p. 24.

11. Ibid., p. 92.

12. [Throughout this section, Agamben quotes from Marx's Economic-Philosophical Manuscripts of 1844. The citations I was able to locate are identified as *MEGA* in the text and refer to *Karl Marx-Friedrich Engels Gesamtausgabe (MEGA)*, vol. 2 (Berlin: Dietz, 1982)—*Trans.*]

13. Moses Hess, *Die letzten Philosophen* (Darmstadt: Leste, 1845), pp. 1–2.

14. This is why Marx does not deny the theological problem, the problem of God as creator of man, but suppresses it much more radically than any atheism, so that he can then say that "atheism . . . makes no more sense, for atheism is a *negation of God*, and posits *man's existence* through this negation; but socialism as socialism has no need for this negation." *MEGA*, p. 398.

15. Friedrich Nietzsche, *The Birth of Tragedy*, trans. Walter Kaufmann (New York: Vintage, 1967), pp. 31–32.

16. Friedrich Nietzsche, *The Will to Power*, trans. Walter Kaufmann and R. J. Hollingdale (New York: Random House, 1967), pp. 7, 3.

17. See ibid., p. 9 n. 2, and p. 17 n. 22.

18. Ibid., p. 17 n. 22.

19. Friedrich Nietzsche, *The Gay Science: With a Prelude in Rhymes*

and an Appendix of Songs, trans. Walter Kaufmann (New York: Vintage, 1974), aphorism 370, pp. 329–331.

20. Nietzsche, *Will to Power,* p. 15 n. 15.

21. Nietzsche, *Gay Science,* aphorism 107, p. 163.

22. Nietzsche, *Will to Power,* p. 452 n. 853.

23. Nietzsche, *Gay Science,* aphorism 109, pp. 167–68.

24. Nietzsche, *Will to Power,* pp. 35–36 n. 55.

25. Friedrich Nietzsche, *Ecce Homo,* trans. J. Hollingdale (New York: Penguin 1992), p. 77.

26. Nietzsche, *Gay Science,* aphorism 276, p. 223.

27. Ibid., aphorism 341, pp. 273–74.

28. Nietzsche, *Will to Power,* aphorism 617, p. 330.

29. Friedrich Nietzsche, *Werke: Kritische Gesamtausgabe,* ed. Giorgio Colli and Mazzino Montinari, vol. 5.2 (New York: de Gruyter, 1973), p. 403.

30. Nietzsche, *Will to Power,* p. 453 n. 853, and p. 435 n. 822.

31. Ibid., pp. 51–52 n. 83.

32. Ibid., p. 225 n. 419. The reading of Marx contained in this chapter would not have been possible without Heidegger's seminal studies on Nietzsche's thought, in particular "The Word of Nietzsche: 'God is dead'" (1950) and *Nietzsche* (1961).

9. The Original Structure of the Work of Art

1. Hölderlin, quoted in Bettina von Arnim, *Die Günderode,* vol. 1 (Leipzig: Insel, 1914), p. 331.

2. Ibid., pp. 333–34.

3. In the first book of the *Metaphysics* (985b), Aristotle, explaining the theory of the atomists, who put emptiness and fullness at the origin and derived all things from them by way of "difference," says that according to Leucippus and Democritus this "difference" had three species— ῥυσμῷ καὶ διαθιγῇ καὶ τροπῇ—and defined rhythm as σχῆμα (from ἔχω), way of holding together, structure.

4. André Lalande, *Vocabulaire technique et critique de la philosophie,* 2d edition, revised and augmented (Paris: Presses Universitaires de France, 1968), p. 1031.

5. It is interesting to note that a similar phenomenon of progressive mathematization of philosophical inquiry was observed by Aristotle. Af-

ter criticizing the platonic theory of ideas and the identification of ideas with numbers, Aristotle comments: "Philosophy has come to be identical with mathematics for modern thinkers, though they say that mathematics is only to be studied as a means to some other end" (Aristotle, *Metaphysics*, trans. W. D. Ross, in *Basic Works of Aristotle*, ed. Richard McKeon [New York: Random House, 1941], 992a, p. 710). According to Aristotle, the reason for this exchange was to be sought in the particular nature of numbers, which is neither sensible nor intelligible but in some way assimilable to a "nonsensible matter."

6. Archilochus, *Fragments*, ed. François Lasserre, French trans. André Bonnard (Paris: Les belles lettres, 1958), frag. 118, p. 39.

7. Martin Heidegger, "What Are Poets For?" in *Poetry, Language, Thought*, p. 118. The careful reader will certainly have noticed how much these pages on the most original dimension of time owe to Heidegger's thought, in particular the paper "Time and Being," in *On Time and Being*, trans. Joan Stambaugh (New York: Harper and Row, 1972).

10. The Melancholy Angel

1. Walter Benjamin, *Einbahnstraße* (One-way street), in *Gesammelte Schriften*, ed. Rolf Tiedemann and Hermann Schweppenhäuser, vol. 4.1, ed. Tillman Rexroth (Frankfurt a.M.: Suhrkamp, 1972), p. 138.

2. In this regard, see Hannah Arendt's remarks in *Men in Dark Times* (New York: Harcourt, Brace and World, 1968), p. 193.

3. It is not difficult to notice that the alienating function of citations corresponds exactly to the alienation produced in criticism by the "readymade" and pop art. Here, too, an object whose meaning was guaranteed by the "authority" of its daily use suddenly uses its traditional intelligibility to become charged with an uncanny power to traumatize. In his article "What Is Epic Theater (ii)," Walter Benjamin defines the characteristic procedure of quotation as "interruption": "To quote a text means to interrupt its context." Walter Benjamin, *Gesammelte Schriften*, vol. 2.2 (Frankfurt a.M: Suhrkamp, 1972), p. 536.

4. It is interesting that Debord, in his search for a "style of negation" as the language of revolutionary subversion, did not notice the implicit destructive potential of quotation. However, the use of "détournement" and plagiarism, which he recommended, plays the same role in his discourse as Benjamin assigned to citation, since "in the positive employment of existing concepts, it includes at the same time the intelligence

of their rediscovered *fluidity* and of their necessary destruction. . . . [In this way] it expresses the domination of present criticism *over its entire past.* . . . [*Détournement*] appears in communication that knows that it cannot lay claim to any guarantee. . . . It is . . . language that no reference to antiquity . . . can confirm." Guy Debord, *La société du spectacle* (Paris: Buchet/Chastel, 1967), pp. 165, 167.

5. That the alienation value later reacquires economic value (and thus exchange value) means nothing other than that in our society alienation fulfills an economically appreciable function.

6. Walter Benjamin, "Theses on the Philosophy of History," in *Illuminations*, ed. Hannah Arendt, trans. Harry Zohn (New York: Schocken, 1969), pp. 257–58.

7. For an iconographic interpretation of Dürer's woodcut, see Erwin Panofsky and Fritz Saxl, *Dürers "Melenconia I," eine quellen- und typengeschichtliche Untersuchung* (Leipzig: B. G. Teubner, 1923), and Walter Benjamin's remarks in *The Origin of the German Tragic Drama*, trans. John Osborne (New York: Verso, 1977), pp. 148–58. The interpretation that I propose does not exclude a purely iconographical one but simply places it in a historical perspective. At any rate, the *typus acediae* from which Dürer's image derives is closely tied, according to Christian theology, to a desperation about man's *status viatoris*, that is, to a loss not of the achievement but of the "path" to the achievement. By embedding the medieval description of sloth in a concrete historico-temporal experience, Dürer made it into the image of the condition of man, who, unable to find tradition and the experience of time inherent in it, is no longer able to find his present space and loses his way in history's linear time.

8. Franz Kafka, *The Blue Octavo Notebooks*, ed. Max Brod, trans. Ernst Kaiser and Eithne Wilkins (Cambridge, Mass.: Exact Change, 1991), p. 15.

9. Franz Kafka, "Reflections on Sin, Pain, Hope, and the True Way," in *The Great Wall of China*, trans. Willa Muir and Edwin Muir (New York: Schocken, 1946), pp. 283, 287.

10. The most penetrating analysis of Kafka's relationship with history can be found in Beda Allemann's essay "Kafka et l'histoire" (in René Char et al., *L'endurance de la pensée: Pour saluer Jean Beaufret* [Plon: Paris, 1968]). One can also find there the interpretation of Kafka's concept of *Standrecht* as "the state of history." We can now put Kafka's image of a state of history side by side with Benjamin's idea of a "now-time" (*Jetztzeit*), understood as a stop in happening, as well as the exigency expressed

in the *Theses on the Philosophy of History*, according to which one should reach a concept of history that corresponds to the fact that the state of emergency is, in fact, the rule.

Rather than speaking of a historical *state*, one should perhaps more properly speak of a historical *ecstasy*. Man is, in fact, incapable of appropriating his historical condition and is therefore always "beside himself" in history.

11. Kafka, *Great Wall of China*, p. 173.

12. Walter Benjamin, letter to Gerhard Scholem, June 12, 1938, in *Briefe*, ed. Gerschom Scholem and Theodor Adorno, vol. 2 (Frankfurt a.M.: Suhrkamp, 1966), p. 763.

13. Franz Kafka, *Tagebücher* 1910–1923, ed. Max Brod (Frankfurt a.M.: Fischer, 1973), journal entry of January 16, 1922, p. 345.

M E R I D I A N

Crossing Aesthetics

Library of Congress Cataloging-in-Publication Data

Agamben, Giorgio
  [Uomo senza contenuto. English]
  The man without content / Giorgio Agamben ; translated by
Georgia Albert.
      p. cm. — (Meridian, crossing aesthetics)
  Includes bibliographical references.
  ISBN 0-8047-3553-0 (hardcover : alk. paper). — ISBN 0-8047-3554-9
(pbk. : alk. paper)
  1. Aesthetics, Modern—20th century. 2. Art—Philosophy.
I. Title. II. Series: Meridian (Stanford, Calif.)
BH201.A413 1999
111'.85—dc21   99-21526

  ⊚ This book is printed on acid-free, recycled paper.

Original printing 1999
Last figure below indicates year of this printing:
08